AUTHENTIC FOOD QUEST

Peru

A Guide to Eat Your Way Authentically Through Lima & Cusco

ROSEMARY KIMANI & CLAIRE ROUGER

Authentic Food Quest Peru
A Guide to Eat Your Way Authentically Through Lima and Cusco

Copyright © 2018 Rosemary Kimani and Claire Rouger

All Rights Reserved
No part of this publication may be reproduced or transmitted in any form or by any means, mechanical or electronic, including photocopying and recording, or by any information storage or retrieval system, without prior written permission of the copyright owners, except for the use of brief quotations in reviews.

ISBN (e-book): 978-0-9978101-2-7
ISBN (paperback): 978-0-9978101-3-4

Editor: Emily Kidd, EmilyKidd.com
Cover and book design: Elena Reznikova, DTPerfect.com

Cover Images Photo Credits:
Authentic Food Quest

Photography by Authentic Food Quest, except where otherwise noted.

Discover Your Food & Travel Profile - Quiz

Do you love food and travel? What kind of food traveler are you? Take our quiz at https://www.authenticfoodquest.com/quiz/ and get your food traveler profile in minutes!

Table of Contents

An Introduction with Cecilia Morote Portella 1
Our Quest for Authentic Food in Peru 3
Our Approach to Authentic Eating in Lima and Cusco 4
How To Use This Book 6

**TERROIR: Learning "The Lay of the Land"
for Authentic Food in Lima and Cusco** 7
- Tips for Food Travelers to Peru 9
- How to Eat Like a Local 12
- How to Shop Like a Local 16

**SAVOR THIS: Top Authentic Peruvian
Foods & Drinks Not To Be Missed** 21
- **Major Cuisine Types in Peru** 21
    Chifa Peruvian-Chinese Cuisine 22
    Criollo: Traditional and Homemade Cuisine 24
    Nikkei: Japanese-Peruvian Cuisine 26

- **Regional Dishes from Peru** 28
    Arequipa Cuisine: Foods & Drinks from the South of Peru 28
    Piura Cuisine: Food and Drinks from the North of Peru 32
    Amazon Cuisine: Food and Drinks from the Peruvian Amazon Jungle .. 34

- **LIMA, PERU** 42
    Authentic Specialties Not to Miss in Lima 45
    Street Food 59
    Desserts 63
    Beverages 67
    Unique Fruits and Produce 75
    Local Markets 81

- **CUSCO, PERU** 84
    Authentic Specialties Not to Miss in Cusco 86
    Beverages 94
    Unique Local Fruits and Produce 101
    Local Markets 109

continued

RESOURCES 113
- Culinary Culture in Peru and Beyond 113
- Health and Fitness While Traveling in Peru 115
- From our Blog: Machu Picchu: The Fulfillment of a Dream 119

ACKNOWLEDGEMENTS 121
ABOUT THE AUTHORS 123

Rosemary and Claire with Cecilia & Mae at Los Piuranos Restaurant, Lima

AN INTRODUCTION
with Cecilia Portella Morote

It's said that the gastronomical culture of any country tells the story of the people. Peru is no exception. Owners of an age old culture, our Peruvian table has adopted forms and essences that have shaped it. Nevertheless, it was also born with its own unique characteristics.

Some people mistakenly believe that those of us who dedicate ourselves to gastronomy are only dedicating ourselves to eating. In fact, this is far from reality. If there's something that motivates us lovers of cuisine, it is to experiment and to know. We are in on a secret: we know that through good food, the flavors and taste of a culture can open before our eyes, before our immediate reality.

This is what Claire and Rosemary do. They pack their luggage and venture out in search of new paths, deciding what to try and what to know. In their quest they made it to Peru, my country, which had a lot to teach them as well.

There's no doubt that the praiseworthy work of researchers and historians fills a fundamental role in solving the question of what sustains our gastronomy, but good food is primarily meant to be experienced. In this book, Rosemary and Claire share their observations and discoveries as they attempt to demonstrate what's behind Peruvian cuisine.

A product of a vast history, generous biodiversity, and creative cooks, Peru's gastronomy is now a notable presence in the world. Foreign fusions provided new elements and techniques, creating a gastronomy rich in a variety of flavors and sensations. That is what we want to show in this publication.

Simply mentioning the best dishes from Peru does not do them justice, since each one has its particular importance. To truly know a country, you must traverse its unique regions. Along the way, you'll come in contact with the history, the flavor and the local people who shape them. Claire and Rosemary had the opportunity to try representative samples of our gastronomy during their time here. Without a doubt they'll need more time to continue enjoying it.

However, the perfect overview they were able to cover left in them the motivation to share the knowledge they gained.

My friend Mae Rivera and I had the opportunity to keep them company in Lima. We watched Claire and Rosemary approach each new flavor we suggested with total openness and natural curiosity: a delightful experience we would repeat over and over again.

One such experience was our encounter with pisco. To understand the full context behind this iconic distillate, Rosemary and Claire had to see behind the scenes. We first ventured to Cerro Azul and spent time on the pier with its calm sea, crisscrossed by the seagulls that swoop across it over and over, eager for a bite of the bounty in our sea. From there we went on to the vineyards, a museum dedicated to Pisco, and on to the marvelous Lunahuaná Valley, two and a half hours south of Lima. Our trip was crowned with a refreshing glass of a classic, traditional, and very Peruvian pisco.

The great biodiversity of the sea inspires the cuisine of our coasts; the Peruvian Amazon informs the exotic dishes of the jungle. In Cusco, the cuisine of the mountains is represented by the potato, while Lima is full of gourmet fusion delicacies. From street food to home cooking, this book is motivated by the unique perspective that Rosemary and Claire have for each dish.

It is a perspective we are grateful for, because for all the world they have traveled so far, Claire and Rosemary have chosen to write about our own Peru.

CECILIA PORTELLA MOROTE
Journalist Specializing in Tourism and Gastronomy

Our Quest for Authentic Food in Peru

It is impossible to offer a complete picture of the depth and breadth of deliciousness across Peru. There is a lifetime of exploration here.

With 492 national dishes, Peru tops the charts in the Guinness Book of World Records for more national dishes than any other country in the world. The variety of flavors and ingredients in Peru is massive.

We cannot cover the entire range of diverse foods in this country. We will, however, give you a taste of what makes this place so special. You'll find cuisines that date back thousands of years, with traditions and new ingredients layered over them.

Each culture that crossed the history of Peru left its touch on the cuisine. The recipes brought by Spanish conquistadors in the 1500s were adopted into local dishes. African and Chinese slaves brought to Peru by the Spaniards and Italians created new lasting dishes. In the mid to late 1800s, Chinese and Japanese immigrants brought their ingredients and culture, and adapted their recipes for local produce.

Regional diversity and years of fusion have created subcategories of unique cuisines, such as the food culture in the Andes and the Amazon, and fusions of Peruvian-Japanese *Nikkei*, and Peruvian-Chinese *chifa*.

This book is not an academic glimpse into regional cuisine; rather, it's an overview of the impressive variety of dishes found in the country, told from our perspective.

At Authentic Food Quest, our goal is to inspire people to explore local flavors on their travels. Too often, tourists only get a cursory introduction to the local food of a region. We believe that by traveling through authentic dishes, people will have a deeper appreciation of the place, the people, and the culture.

Whether you're a newcomer or a seasoned visitor, exploring these local dishes will give you a better appreciation of Peru, and what makes the food and the country so special.

...

Our Approach to Authentic Eating in Lima and Cusco

To understand the local flavors of a region, we travel slowly and live like locals. At Authentic Food Quest, we immerse ourselves completely into a culture by connecting with people as we explore the culinary delights of the markets, restaurants, and festivals where they live.

As foreigners, we ask a lot of questions about the food and local food culture. We want to know the rituals behind eating certain dishes at certain times, the reasons specific combinations go together, and the stories behind the beverages that wash everything down.

These "beginner" questions force locals to analyze their own routines and habits. As a result, their responses are filled with rich insights about their local food and culture.

At **AuthenticFoodQuest.com** we tell the stories of local specialties and flavors not to miss in a particular country or region. Traditional foods have deep cultural significance, and they offer a glimpse into the rich local life that created them. On our site and in this book, we bring that perspective to bear.

We don't just eat good food (although that's the best part); we use a 12-step approach to discover local flavors. Our "Savor Local" method breaks down into four main components: researching, connecting with locals, experiencing the unique and local dishes, and finally, interviewing local experts.

1. We start out by researching the local foods ahead of time. We do extensive online research, reading articles, blog posts and books about the food. (Lucky for you, we've distilled that research in this guide!)
2. We connect with locals prior to leaving, and also while in the country. This is how we met Food Journalist Cecilia Portella Morote in Peru. Generally, all the locals we meet are open and proudly share their favorite authentic dishes with us. In addition, they tell stories, memories, and the best places to experience the dishes.
3. We visit numerous farmers' markets and local food stores to see the produce in season as well as the unique and regional specialties. We sample and eat the local specialties at eateries and restaurants that focus on the regional and authentic dishes.
4. We interview local experts who help us understand the local specialties and their cultural significance. These experts include vendors at the farmers' markets, restaurant owners and chefs as well as locals we meet along our journey.

    In the following pages, you will find the emblematic dishes, desserts, and traditional drinks of Peru. We have focused specifically on our explorations of Lima and Cusco, the two most visited destinations in Peru.

    You will also find an overview of the cuisine and how to experience Peruvian cuisine like a local. Interspersed throughout the book are stories, tips and fun facts about the regional dishes. We include a list of unique local food activities such as tours, and food festivals to enhance your overall experience.

    Think of this book as a complement to your travel guide. Most guides present a cursory overview on the local dishes. Here you get an exclusive focus on the authentic and regional specialties.

    In Peru, every dish has a story. In this book, you will not only get an introduction to Peruvian food; you'll also explore the history of how this unique gastronomy came to be.

BUEN PROVENCHO!

How To Use This Book

This book is broken into three main parts:

1. TERROIR

TERROIR provides a "lay of the land" of what to expect on your culinary trip in Peru.

- You will find a summary of Peruvian cuisine to help orient you to this wonderful gastronomy.
- Food related tips are also provided, including how to eat and drink safely in the country.
- Learn where to eat and shop like the locals, and discover the different kinds of eateries and local markets to be found.
- This part ends with an overview of the local food stores and the Mistura Festival—the largest food festival in Latin America.

2. SAVOR THIS: LIMA & CUSCO

SAVOR THIS – LIMA & CUSCO dives into the local flavors you must not miss.

- **LIMA** - What and Where to Eat in Lima.
- **CUSCO** - What and Where to Eat in Cusco
- In each of these sections you will find the local and traditional specialties broken down into dishes, desserts, street food, local beverages and unique produce.
- In this section you will also find unique tips from experts we interviewed, and links to videos with locals discussing some of the traditional specialties on our website, AuthenticFoodQuest.com.

3. RESOURCES

RESOURCES contains additional necessary odds and ends for making your trip a success.

- We showcase top local chefs who are instrumental in putting Peruvian cuisine on the culinary map.
- As devoted culinary explorers, we are also devoted to keeping fit and staying active. We have included travel fitness pointers for both Lima and Cusco.
- The story of Peru would not complete without talking about Machu Picchu. Find a short excerpt from our website at AuthenticFoodQuest.com about the *Fulfillment of a Dream*.

In the end, this book provides a written and visual record of some of the local flavors to savor in Peru. The richness and the flavors of Peru are vast. The local food experiences are innumerable. Use this as a guide to open up to the fascinating culture of Peru.

1. TERROIR

*Learning "The Lay of the Land"
for Authentic Food in Lima and Cusco*

Welcome To Peru

Peru is a landscape of diversity and drama. Ranging from desert to tropics to mountain highlands, Peru includes 30 of the world's 32 climates.

The *Costa* (coast) on the western edge includes the narrow coastal plains between the ocean and the Andes. The *Sierra* (highlands) rises up into the Andes mountain range, which extends from the north to the southeast of the country. The *Selva* (jungle) lies to the east, encompassing the Amazon rainforest.

At 31 million inhabitants in 2015, Peru's population makes it the third largest country in South America after Brazil and Argentina.

**Peru
Three Zones**

Costa
Atacama Desert
(driest in the world)

Sierra
Andes (2nd highest mountains in world)

Selva
Amazon (largest tropical rainforest in world)

Peruvian Cuisine

This very distinct geography has influenced the development of Peruvian cuisine. The varied landscapes within Peru provide for a wide range of ingredients and diversity of cooking styles.

The cuisine is heavily influenced by the climate and microclimates in each of the main regions. A generous abundance of fish and seafood comes from the Humboldt Current that flows off Peru's Pacific Coastline. Combined with staples such as potatoes, corn, squash and grains from the mountain ranges, the unique dishes of Peru reflect the close proximity of these environments.

Foreigners have also evolved the cuisine of the country. Spanish, African, Chinese, Japanese, and Italian influences each made their mark as these groups arrived with their own unique products, customs or techniques. Out of a union of many gastronomies, Peru is one of the world's original fusion cuisines.

Today, Peru continues to create some of the world's most innovative and exciting cuisines. Peru won the World's Leading Culinary Destination for five years in a row between 2012 and 2016.

Different regions of Peru use local produce that is specific to the area. A tour of the colorful stands of vegetables and exotic fruit at the farmers' markets is a delight, in addition to the dishes made with them. While the focus of this book is on Lima and Cusco, you will find the best of different regions of Peru represented in these cities. Use the **Savor This** section of the book to familiarize yourself with the local flavors, including addresses of where you can find and try these specialties.

The notoriety of Peru as a leading culinary destination can be attributed to Gastón Acurio, the superstar chef who put Peruvian cuisine on the map. Considered the father of modern Peruvian cuisine, Acurio has turned Peruvian food into the country's proudest export. In the **Resources** section, we highlight other superstar chefs who are also raising the gastronomy profile of Peru, and shaping the future of this culinary gem.

Tips for Food Travelers to Peru

Food is revered in Peru and locals take the time to enjoy and savor their food. Meals traditionally are eaten three times a day. Breakfast or *desayuno* is normally eaten between 7:00 am and 9:00 am. Lunch or *almuerzo*, is the main meal of the day. In the later afternoon, about 5:30 pm or 6:00 pm, Peruvians eat a quick snack or meal called *lonche*. This can be a savory snack such as *tamales* or something as simple as bread with butter, ham, cheese or jam. And dinner or *cena* is usually smaller and lighter than the lunchtime meal.

The Lunch Time Menu

In Peru, *almuerzo* (lunch) is the main meal of the day. Restaurants both large and small offer lunchtime specials, known in Spanish as *menú del día*. The menu typically consists of a starter, a main course and a drink, sometimes with a small dessert.

Lunch special at El Bijao Restaurant, Lima

Note, lunch is also the time to eat *ceviche*, a specialty dish of marinated seafood. It is still considered quite fresh and is typically not eaten later in the day.

The prices range depending on the city and where you are eating lunch. In upscale neighborhoods in Lima, prices will run about S/.10 nuevos soles (US $3). Whereas in smaller cities or at the local market, expect to pay about S/.5 (US $1.50).

You should certainly not judge Peruvian cuisine by the low-priced offerings; you'll get healthy portions and incredibly tasty flavors.

Water

Generally speaking, tap water in Peru is not safe to drink. At both homes in Cusco and Lima where we stayed, there was a pitcher of boiled water always available.

While everyone used tap water for bathing and showering, we would use boiled water for brushing our teeth and drinking.

Buying bottled water is the most straightforward way of ensuring water safety. Unfortunately this results in the excessive use of plastic and pollution. While there are attempts at recycling efforts in the country, you will still find discarded plastic bottles all around.

Authentic Food Quest has partnered with GRAYL (**www.thegrayl.com**) to provide ultra-light purifier bottles to our readers. With just one press and in under 15 seconds, water from virtually any source can be purified against a variety of chemicals, viruses and heavy metals.

When you use the discount code **AFQ-WATER** at checkout from Grayl.com, you will receive **20% OFF** your purchases.

Enjoy your culinary travels in Peru with clean and purified drinking water.

Tipping

The culture of tipping in Peru is not as ingrained as it is in the U.S. or Europe. However, that does not necessarily mean that tipping is not appreciated.

At many upscale restaurants, gratuity is added as a service charge and is about 10% of your bill.

At more low-key restaurants, eateries or street vendors, tipping is not common, nor is it automatically included in the bill.

However, if you've enjoyed your meal and service, leaving a *propina* (tip) of about S/.2 to S/.10 (US $0.60 – $3) is perfectly appropriate, depending on the cost of the meal and size of your group.

Eating Safely in Peru

Intriguing delights are available across Peru, from the streets, to markets, to traditional restaurants and more. Generally the food is safe, but you do want to exercise caution.

To eat or not to eat *ceviche* (raw fish), is one of the questions that comes up often among visitors to Peru. In this case, we do what the locals do. *Ceviche* is typically made from the fresh catch of the day. Locals will tell you that the best time for *ceviche* is at lunchtime when the fish is still fresh. Save yourself any anxiety and avoid *ceviche* at any other time of the day.

Locals queuing up for anticuchos, Lima

Here are the top takeaways for exploring this food paradise safely.

10 Food Safety Tips for Peru

1. Give yourself time to adjust before trying all the new and exotic foods.
2. Observe where and when the locals eat and adopt the local eating rhythm.
3. Stay away from tap water and use bottled or filtered water.
4. Choose prepared food that is cooked and served hot.
5. Wash your hands before eating or handling food.
6. Wash fruits and vegetables prior to eating them.
7. Ask the locals for recommendations. Everyone has their favorite *cevichería* or local spot.
8. When buying juices, make sure the vendor is using bottled water.
9. When in doubt, use your own cutlery to ensure hygiene. We always carry a spork (spoon-fork combo) on our travels.
10. Choose to eat at street vendors, market stalls and local restaurants that are busy and have a high turnover of food.

Exercise caution, but don't let that stop you from enjoying the culinary delights of Peru.

Eating Vegetarian in Peru

All major cities and towns have a local market usually close to the main square. This is one of the best places for vegetarians to immerse themselves and see Peru`s grand diversity of products. You'll find a fantastic range of unique fruits and grains that will please most vegetarians.

As a major tourist destination, Peru is becoming more and more familiar with vegetarianism and even veganism. You will find some organic markets, though the products are similar to what you'll find at a local restaurant for a fraction of the price.

Nevertheless, new restaurants are opening all the time that cater to those who don't eat animals and animal products. Many of them are geared toward foreigners, and you will see some authentic potato- and quinoa-based dishes found in this book.

Another great resource for vegetarian restaurants across Peru is the website **HappyCow.net**, which lists vegetarian and vegan restaurants and stores across the country.

Here are few helpful phrases for your trip:
- *Yo soy vegetariano/a.* (I'm a vegetarian.)
- *Yo soy vegano/a.* (I'm vegan.)
- *Yo no como carne, queso, huevos o leche.* (I don't eat meat, cheese, eggs or milk.)
- *Voy a tener la ensalada de frutas por favor.* (I'll have the fruit salad, please.)

How To Eat Like a Local

Peru offers a variety of eating establishments. The cost is determined to a large extent by the quality and location, ranging from street foods, fast foods and local farmers' markets to mid-range restaurants, all the way up to gastronomy establishments. Tourist-oriented destinations like Miraflores will put a large dent in your wallet versus colorful and affordable local finds.

To sample a wide range of experiences, we encourage you to eat at the variety of establishments available.

Street food vendors offer a quick bite or snack straight off the hot pot or grill.

Local markets provide freshly prepared locals meals served under a *menú del día*, or daily lunch special.

In-between restaurants and markets are *huariques*. These are little family restaurants that offer traditional home cooked meals without much fanfare.

Picanterías are similar to *huariques* in that they are traditional restaurants predominantly in and around the cities of Arequipa and Cusco.

Gastronomy restaurants offer high-end experiences for ten times and more the prices of a meal offered in the markets.

Local Farmers' Markets

Local farmers' markets are fascinating experiences, and they are some of the best places to understand the local cuisine and produce of a region.

Throughout Peru you will find countless markets of different styles. From neighborhood restaurants to covered and outdoor markets, the size varies from large to small. Regardless of the type of

Locals eating at Mercado Surquillo, Lima

market, you'll find an overwhelming abundance of exotic fruits and produce, meats, poultry, fish and more.

Markets also serve food and are popular lunchtime destinations amongst locals for a quick and cheap meal. No matter the size or set-up of the market, you will find counters to pull up a chair and home cooks offering the special *menú del día.*

The food at the local markets consists of traditional Peruvian dishes accompanied with a local drink. The food is made fresh and is quite delicious. The menu typically consists of a starter, which is often soup, followed by the main dish and a watered-down fruit juice.

At the time of our visit to Peru, eating at the farmers' markets was approximately 5 Peruvian Nuevos Soles (PEN), or about $1.50 USD.

Huariques

A *huarique* (also spelled "*warique*") is a type of family restaurant that offers traditional food and typical dishes from the region. They are typically not fancy places, but rather eateries where ordinary people can enjoy a simple, home-cooked meal. They are also somewhat secret places that are not advertised. People learn about them via word of mouth.

The Spanish word *huarique* actually comes from two words of the Quechua language: "*wa,*" which means hidden or secret, and "*rique,*" which means a stew. Hence, a *huarique* is a secret place that serves good food.

At a *huarique*, you will find families dedicated to cooking who are well known for one or two signature dishes. The quality of the food rivals what is found at high-end restaurants, with the difference being the price.

These are some of the best places to eat in Peru.

Picanterías

A *picantería* is a typical eatery found in countryside of Peru. Before commercial restaurants as we know them today, *picanterías* were known as improvised dining rooms in private homes who opened their doors for the field workers in the area.

Customers would walk through the kitchen and see and taste what was being cooked before ordering. Although "*picante*" means "spicy food," not all dishes served at a *picantería* are necessarily spicy.

Accompanying the traditional food are local drinks and homemade beverages. You will likely find homemade beers like *chicha de jora* (see the **Beverages** of Cusco section) and others depending on the region.

Picanteria Arequipa, Lima

Picanterías are the perfect places to taste flavors, ingredients, and seasonings of the region. The food is rustic, yet beautifully cooked and presented. Locals usually order the dish of the day. You will find big flavors that can rival any typical gourmet restaurant.

Gastronomy Restaurants

Lima is a city experiencing a culinary renaissance, with growing local pride in its booming restaurant scene. Chefs trained in some of the top culinary schools around the world have returned to Peru to apply their new skills and techniques to the vast treasure-trove of traditional recipes.

The Andes and Peruvian Amazon jungle are home to countless kinds of exotic, little-known but utterly delicious herbs, fruits and vegetables to draw from. The frigid Humboldt Current provides a myriad of seafood specialties from the Pacific Ocean. Chefs in Peru have access to just about every kind of ecosystem to draw from.

The most famous high-end restaurant that is at the core of Peru's gastronomic rebirth is **Astrid & Gastón**, which opened in 1994. This flagship project of chef Gastón Acurio and his German chocolatier wife Astrid Gutsche (who was herself once named the world's best pastry chef) is at the top of every must-visit restaurant list in Peru.

Chef Virgilio Martínez Véliz of **Central** is currently the biggest name in Peruvian cuisine. He unearths ingredients from every corner of Peru, drawing from communities along the coast, mountains and rainforest, and featuring ingredients from the fish and seafood below sea level to altitudes as high as 12,000 feet. The cuisine takes diners on a culinary journey up, over and under Peru.

At **Maido**, chef Mitsuharu Tsumura pays tribute to the country's diversity through delicious *Nikkei* cuisine. Read more about Peruvian-Japanese *Nikkei* cuisine in the **Major Cuisine Types in Peru** section.

In San Pellegrino's 2017 ranking of the world's 50 best restaurants, Lima was the only city to have two eateries in the top 10. Central received fifth place, Maido ranked eighth, and Astrid & Gastón placed at #33. Together with many up-and-coming chefs, these establishments are at the forefront of the Peruvian culinary movement.

Other notable high-end restaurants include **La Mar**, the second flagship eatery from Gastón Acurio. "La Mar" translates to "the high seas"; this restaurant offers a variety of *ceviches* and numerous other versions of Peru's many original fish and shellfish classics.

This restaurant list is by no means comprehensive and is not designed to feature all of Lima's best restaurants. We've highlighted a slice of some of the notable chefs and restaurants that are shaping Peru's culinary renaissance.

How to Shop Like a Local

 Local Markets

The local farmers' markets in Peru are a must-visit destination to explore the range of Peruvian cuisine. Larger markets have extensive selections of over 3,000 native potatoes of the country. You'll see shapes, colors and sizes that are unimaginable.

Native grains like quinoa—also known as the "Golden Grain of the Andes"—are on display. Depending on where they are grown, you will see quinoa seeds range in color from black to red, white to yellow, and any shade in between.

The Amazon rainforest makes up about 60% of the country, and it is one of the last true frontiers on earth, creating incredible diversity in the cuisine.

One of our favorite discoveries was the strange Amazonian fruits at the market. At Surquillo farmers' market in Lima, we were blown away by fruits with unusual shapes and pungent smells.

Read more in the **Unique Local Fruits** of Lima section.

Be sure to visit the local markets in the your neighborhood on your travels to Peru.

Mercado Surquillo No.1, Lima

 ## Supermarkets

The traditional way of shopping for fresh fruits, vegetables, meats and groceries is by going to the local *mercado* (market). In addition, large supermarkets are convenient places to pick up food, snacks, beer and wine. Most locals shop at the market, where the prices are often cheaper, though the supermarkets are an efficient way of shopping.

 ## Plaza Vea

This is the largest supermarket chain in Peru. You will find a wide variety of local and imported products at good prices. Plaza Vea was the most convenient supermarket near us and our favorite stop for dried goods, fresh dairy products and beverages.

 ## Wong Supermarket

Wong Supermarket is another large supermarket chain with a dominant presence in Lima. It was run by Chinese immigrants until it was recently acquired by a Chilean corporation. They have 14 stores all around Lima and they offer a vast selection of products and great service.

If you're looking for imported products and willing to pay the price, Wong Supermarket offers a wide range of imported products.

Vivanda

Vivanda is an upscale supermarket with a broad selection of imported products. The prices are higher than at other supermarkets. Most locations have a small space where you can have a seat and enjoy lunch or a coffee, and most offer free WIFI access.

Metro

Metro is part of the Wong chain of food stores. The great selection of products and affordable prices makes it very popular with locals. Metro carries their own brand of high-quality products.

Tottus

This supermarket chain is part of the Chilean Falabella family of stores with a presence in Chile and Peru. You'll find a good selection of food, wines, and fresh produce. In 2017, Tottus opened one of their supermarkets in Cusco, in the district of San Sebastián.

Bakeries

The history of bread can be traced back to the Inca period where it was made with corn. Today, bread in Peru is a common fixture at most tables at breakfast and with meals.

Different regions of the country have different types of bread, and freshly baked loaves come in all shapes and textures; some are sweet and others are salty. Special breads like *tanta wawa* are eaten for religious festivals. And in Lima, you'll find a Peruvian French-style bread.

There is one particular bread that is famous and much loved: *pan chapla*. This bread is typical of the Ayacucho region in south-central Peru, on the eastern slopes of the Andes Mountains.

Pan chapla is round in shape and resembles a pita. This beautiful bread is flavorful and made with the simple ingredients: salt, flour, sugar, anise and yeast.

We fondly recall our first morning in Cusco, where were had freshly baked *pan chapla* with breakfast. The simplicity and intensity of flavors is the perfect start to the day.

In the Lince neighborhood of Lima where we stayed, we discovered quinoa bread. You can read more about this in the **Unique Produce** from the Andes section.

There are more than 400 different types of breads consumed across the country, so no matter what part of the country you are visiting, be sure to stop in stop into a local bakery and sample the traditional bread of the region.

 ## Food Festivals in Lima

Peru hosts numerous festivals throughout the country: some are particular to a certain region or city, and others are celebrated throughout the country.

Peruvians celebrate Incan and Catholic holidays with equal fervor. Because many citizens have both Spanish and indigenous ancestry, there is a never-ending series of moments to celebrate.

Neighborhood food festival, Lima

When it comes to food, the most important celebration is the Mistura Festival, which takes place in Lima.

 ## Mistura

Peruvian restaurants and famous chefs from around the world gather in Lima celebrate Peruvian cuisine each autumn for Latin America's biggest food festival. The word *mistura* means "mixture" in Portuguese, and the cuisine served at Mistura reflects a fusion of cultural dishes.

There are three main hallmarks of the festival. The first is the presence of Peru's top chefs: people come from all over the world to salivate over the newest in food trends and demonstrations from chefs like Virgilio Martinez of Central in Lima, and Gastón Acurio, the Peruvian chef with restaurants throughout Latin America and Europe.

The sprawling farmers' market called El Gran Mercado is a favorite. Over 300 farmers from around Peru showcase the products of their region. Visitors can try some of the thousands of potato varieties grown in Peru, multicolored quinoa, coffee, spices and more.

The third hallmark is Pisco Hall, where the country's national drink is celebrated in all variations. Watch grape-stomping dance demonstrations or try a handcrafted pisco sour. Vineyards have stalls where curious travelers can buy a tasting, with sample bottles of pisco available for purchase.

Our favorite quote from Gastón Acurio describes the the country's greatest passion.

> *"Peru is the only country in the whole world where food is the most important thing. If you go to Brazil, it's soccer. If you go to Colombia, it's music. But in Peru, the most important source of pride is food."*

2. SAVOR THIS
Top Authentic Peruvian Foods & Drinks Not To Be Missed

MAJOR CUISINE TYPES IN PERU
- Chifa: Peruvian-Chinese Cuisine
- Criollo: Traditional and Homemade Cuisine
- Nikkei: Japanese-Peruvian Cuisine

REGIONAL DISHES FROM ACROSS PERU IN LIMA
- Arequipa Cuisine: Food and Drinks from the South of Peru
- Piura Cuisine: Food and Drinks from the North of Peru
- Amazon Cuisine: Food and Drinks from the Peruvian Amazon Jungle

Major Cuisine Types in Peru

Peruvian food is a beautiful confluence of cultures. As we saw in the introduction, Peruvian dishes have heavy influences not only from Spanish colonists, but also African slaves and Chinese and Japanese immigrants. This has created a gastronomic experience like no other.

This section introduces you to three major cuisines and the typical dishes within each cuisine type. Some of the dishes are not designated to a specific cuisine, but have become part of the Peruvian food culture identity. We give an overview of those dishes here, and you can find greater depth and detail on the top dishes in the **Authentic Specialties** section for Lima.

🍴 Chifa: Peruvian-Chinese Cuisine

The sheer number of Chinese restaurants will be hard to miss in Lima: you can find a *chifa* restaurant literally on every corner. You can recognize them by their signature ornate fronts, usually in red and green with beautiful dragons.

The Chinese have a long history in Peru. They were the first Asians to arrive in Peru between 1848 and 1874. These early immigrants came as laborers, with most staying and establishing small businesses and restaurants. Barrio Chino de Lima is one of the Western hemisphere's earliest Chinatowns.

Peru has the most Chinese restaurants in South America, and it is only in Peru that Chinese food is referred to as *chifa*. Unlike in the U.S., where Chinese food is considered "ethnic", *chifa* is so deeply integrated with Peru and the food that is has become, in itself, Peruvian.

In Chinese, "chi" means to eat and "fan" means rice. This is the origin of the famous Chinese-Peruvian cuisine.

The Chinese introduced new ingredients such as ginger, soy sauce and scallions while maintaining their traditional cooking methods. They also used local ingredients like sweet pineapples and bananas from the Amazon and potatoes from the Andes highlands to create *chifa* cuisine.

Five Must-Try Chifa Dishes

#1: Arroz Chaufa

Also known as just *chaufa*, *arroz chaufa* is the most emblematic of the *chifa* dishes. The word *chaufa* comes from Cantonese and literally means "fried rice." It is a simple dish, prepared with a mix of fried rice, vegetables, Chinese onions, garlic, ginger, eggs, and chicken, cooked in a wok with soy sauce. It can also be pre-

Arroz Chaufa, Chinese–Peruvian fried rice, Lima

pared with other meats such as pork and steak. It is said to have been created by Chinese slaves who put any leftovers on rice. Cooks who specialize in the art of making *chaufa* have their own name: they are called *chauferos*.

#2: Chaufa De Marisco

This variation of *chaufa* is prepared with seafood. *Chaufa* is so much a part of the Peruvian food culture that it is not only reserved for *chifa* restaurants; we tried *chaufa de marisco* at a *cevichería* at the Surquillo farmers' market.

Chaufa is prepared with *ají amarillo* (yellow chili pepper), rice, calamari and shrimp. The dish gets its nice yellow color from the seafood and the *ají amarillo*. The flavors and fresh seafood make it much more interesting. We recommend skipping the standard *arroz chaufa* and going straight for the *chaufa de marisco*.

#3: Lomo Saltado

While the roots of this beef stir fry are Chinese, *lomo saltado* is considered a traditional Peruvian dish. We describe this quintessential Peruvian meal in more detail in the **Authentic Specialties** of Lima section. Try it at a *chifa* restaurant and enjoy both the fusion of flavors and environment.

#4: Sopa Wantán

Sopa Wantán, also spelled *Sopa Wonton*, is the most common soup served in the chifa. It is usually offered at lunch or with dinner. It is a simple soup made of noodles, meat-filled wontons, cilantro, Chinese onion and chicken. Quite basic but full of flavors, it's an enjoyable soup to stimulate your appetite prior to your meal.

#5: Tallarín Saltado de Pollo

Along with *chaufa*, *tallarín* is one of the dishes on every *chifa*'s menu. *Tallarín* are yellow noodles made with eggs. They are most commonly prepared with chicken (*tallarín con pollo*). Similarly to the *chaufa*, the *tallarín* is stir-fried in a wok with vegetables, Chinese onions, chicken, soy sauce and ginger. There are several variations of this dish with a wide range of vegetables and meats.

🍴 Criollo: Traditional and Homemade Cuisine

Criollo dishes are comfort foods: they're the everyday meals that Peruvians eat in their homes.

Criollo is often confused with creole, but in Peru it means something different. In Peru, Criollo refers to the people raised in the coast, mostly in Lima, and are descendants of the Spanish colonial settlers. Criollo dishes are foods one's grandmother from Spain would cook, but with Peruvian ingredients. For example, *arroz con mariscos* would be equivalent to *paella Peruana*. Many of the dishes are found in the coastal and central regions of Peru where the early immigrants first settled.

This style of cuisine mixes native Peruvian ingredients and Spanish cooking techniques with additions from African, Chinese and Japanese cultures. It is so popular and iconic that you'll find every dish on the following list in the **Authentic Specialties** or **Street Foods** sections for Lima.

Five Must-Try Criollo Dishes

#1: Ají de Gallina

Ají de gallina is one of the most typical native Peruvian dishes. This fusion of Spanish and Quechua ingredients uses *ají amarillo* (or yellow chili pepper) to add flavor to the food. This is typically boiled potatoes or rice served with succulent chicken in a creamy, flavorful sauce. See more on this dish in the **Authentic Specialties** of Lima section.

#2: Causa

Causa is a very unique Peruvian starter made of potatoes. Not just any potatoes, but Andean potatoes. Potatoes originated in Peru, and there are more than 3000 varieties. Some people say *causa* comes from the Quechua word *kausay* (sustenance of life). There are endless ways to compose and present this signature dish. The two most typical classics are *causa limeña* and *causa rellena*. See more in the **Authentic Specialties** section for Lima.

#3: Anticuchos
Anticuchos come from the African slaves who were brought to Peru by the Spanish in the 16th century. The most traditional is the *anticuchos de corazon*, which are pieces of grilled beef heart. The **Street Food** section goes into more detail about this much-loved delicacy.

#4: Lomo Saltado
As mentioned in the **Chifa Cuisine** and **Authentic Specialties** sections, *lomo saltado* is one of the most emblematic and traditional dishes in Peru. You'll find it at restaurants, farmers' markets, or in the kitchens of locals.

Delightful Lomo Saltado

#5: Tacu Tacu
This typical Peruvian dish owes its heritage to the Afro-Peruvian communities. The ingenious way of using leftover rice and beans in a savory combination is both interesting and delicious. Read more about *tacu tacu* in the **Authentic Specialties** section.

🍴 Nikkei: Japanese-Peruvian Cuisine

You may not be aware, but Peru has the second largest Japanese population in South America after Brazil. In fact, Peru was the first country in South America to set up diplomatic relations with Japan and accept immigrants. At the end of the 19th century, when Japan was pushing farmers to emigrate, 790 Japanese pioneers migrated to Peru with the promise of farm jobs.

The Japanese immigrants worked in the fields, mainly in sugarcane plantations, and later on settled in the cities opening their own small businesses. The Japanese started integrating with Peruvians, bringing their culinary heritage and their own techniques. *Nikkei* cuisine was born as a result of the fusion of Japanese recipes and traditions with Peruvian ingredients.

The Japanese introduced new ingredients to Peruvian cuisine: miso, ginger, soy, wasabi and rice vinegar joined the traditional Peruvian ingredients such as *ají* (yellow pepper), Andean potatoes and corn. This fusion of the two cuisine cultures didn't happen overnight; it took place progressively. Today, *Nikkei* cuisine is constantly evolving. The best way to understand it is by experiencing it in the many *Nikkei* restaurants of Lima.

Five Must-Try Nikkei Dishes

#1: Amazon Nikkei

Japanese fusion or *Nikkei* cuisine extends to the Amazon Jungle. Amazon *Nikkei* incorporates slices of a fish from the Amazon called *paiche* (pronounced pie-chay). The other ingredients are a creative mix of Japanese and Peruvian blends: *anticucho* dressing, white miso *causa*, *chonta* salad and cocona-and-mirin vinaigrette.

#2: Ceviche Nikkei

As mentioned previously, *ceviche* is a part of Peru's national heritage. *Ceviche Nikkei* takes a different approach to preparing the dish. Traditional Peruvian *ceviche* calls for long hours of marinating fresh fish in lime juice until it is "cooked", while the *Nikkei* approach is much faster. Lime is added only a few minutes right before serving, to keep the fish from "overcooking." Ginger and soy sauce are added for additional flavor.

#3: El Barranquino

While exploring the Barranco district of Lima, we stumbled upon a *Nikkei* restaurant called Hosso Sushi and Cebiches Bar. Here we ordered one of their classic *Nikkei* specialties called "El Barranquino". On a black platter, we were served five slices of salmon balanced delicately on a bed of *camote* (sweet potato) purée, with a touch of wasabi. On the side was a salsa made with cocona, a fruit from the Amazon jungle.

At first glance, five pieces of salmon did not seem like it would be enough. However when combined with the sweet potato purée, this dish ended up being much more filling than expected. The sweet and spicy salsa was refreshing and helped balance the taste of the sweet potatoes. In short, this was a delicious example of the fusion of Japanese Peruvian cultures.

#4: Pancayaki

One of the classic dishes in traditional *Nikkei* cuisine is this re-interpreted *maki* roll. These rolls use local ingredients such as native Andean potatoes. Other ingredients you'll find include avocados, onion tempura, octopus, *anticuchera* sauce and mushrooms with the native Andean potatoes sprinkled on top.

Pancayaki

#5: Tiradito

Tiradito is one of the dishes that most reflects the Japanese influence on Peruvian cuisine. It is a dish of raw fish which is thinly cut, giving it the appearance of carpaccio or sashimi. Like sashimi, *tiradito* is served raw and usually prepared immediately after ordering.

Regional Dishes from Peru

The diversity of native foods in Peru is unmatched, and the fusion of the different cultures has made each ingredient shine in the culinary landscape.

It is impossible, especially for visitors, to eat the local cuisine in every single region of the country. Fortunately, Lima is the country's the gastronomic capital, and is a great place to discover the large variety of Peruvian cuisines.

In this section we profile the local cuisine from the South of Peru, the North of the Peru and the Peruvian Amazon Jungle, each represented in restaurants in Lima.

We were accompanied to each of these restaurants by our food-loving *limeñas*: Cecilia, Mae and Patricia, our Airbnb host. Each of these restaurants were carefully selected for having the best and most representative food from the different regions.

The gastronomy in each of the regions is rich with influences from immigrants, the terroir and the climate. Although we did not have a chance to travel to the different regions, the dishes outlined here will introduce you to some of the local dishes, desserts and drinks.

Enjoy these little bites of the different regions across Peru.

Arequipa Cuisine: Foods & Drinks from the South of Peru

Peruvians joke that you need a different passport to enter Arequipa, Peru's second largest city.

The rivalry around food between *limeños* (people from Lima) and *arequipeños* (people from Arequipa) is undeniable in Peru. Even though Arequipa is only about one-tenth the size of Lima, it is equal in terms of cuisine, historical significance, confidence and pride.

The rivalry between Lima and Arequipa is so fierce that Arequipa has continuously attempted to gain independence from Peru and create an Independent Republic of Arequipa. Arequipa even has its own flag and national anthem.

Traditional food from Arequipa is served in restaurants known as *picanterías*, which only serve certain dishes on certain days. For example, on Monday they serve *chaque de tripas* (tripe soup); on Tuesday they offer *chairo* (beef, dried lamb and potato stew). *Chupe de camarones* (shrimp chowder) is reserved for Saturday, and on Sunday it's *adobo* pork stew. *Picanterías* usually feature regional musical groups or singers.

In the company of Patricia, our Airbnb host, we went to La Estrellita del Sur Picantería in Lima to discover the remarkable Arequipa dishes. While waiting for our meal, Patricia (who is from Lima) shared stories with us about Arequipeños and their pride.

At La Estrellita del Sur Picantería, we had two emblematic dishes and drinks, and one traditional dessert. There are certainly a lot of more traditional dishes we did not explore; Arequipa is said to have over 194 dishes registered.

In this section we invite you to discover just a few of the local dishes and drinks typical of Arequipa.

#1: Rocoto Relleno with Pastel de Papa

This is a delicious and traditional dish of Arequipa. It begins with a chili pepper (resembling a bell pepper) stuffed with beef and a mixture of garlic, onion, olives and sometimes hard boiled eggs, and soft melted cheese. *Rocoto relleno* is traditionally served with a side of *pastel de papa*: four to six layers of sliced potatoes with melted cheese oozing from every layer. We talk more about *rocoto relleno* in the **Authentic Specialties** of Cusco section.

Rocoto Relleno with Pastel de Papa

#2: Chupe de Camarones

Chupe de camarones is a decadent shrimp chowder featuring large *camarones* from the river. These are large-sized shrimps are not deshelled, which means removing the shrimp shells and shucking the shrimp as you eat.

The thick soup has a cream base and a cacophony of other ingredients including potatoes, squash, rice, lima beans, carrots, corn milk, eggs, salt and *huacatay* (local aromatic herbs).

With the huge shrimp and exquisite tastes, the flavors and textures are amazing. This is one incredibly tasty and filling soup that needs to be experienced.

The soup was served in a large bowl which made it perfect for sharing.

#3: Queso Helado Dessert

Queso helado translates directly to "cheese ice cream," though the name doesn't refer to the ingredients. Instead, you'll be sucking on a block of sweet ice with milk, coconut, cloves and cinnamon. The name comes from the traditional preparation, where the dessert looks more like sliced cheese rather than scoops of ice-cream. Arequipa is known to be the birthplace of this artisanal ice-cream.

Amazing cheese ice cream with Arequipa flag

Traditional Arequipa Drinks

#1: Chicha de Jora

One of the most traditional drinks in Arequipa is *chicha de jora*. Read more about this traditional home-brewed beer in the **Beverages** of Cusco section.

We highlight it here because of the large role *chicha de jora* plays in Arequipa culture. *Picanterías* had their start as *chicherías*, gathering spots where locals would get together to drink *chicha de jora*. Then food started being served and over time, *chicherías* evolved into *picanterías*.

#2: Kola Escocesa

"*Kola Escocesa,*" which translates to "Scottish Cola," is a fruity Arequipan soft drink that is not excessively sweet (as compared to Inca Kola, the other famous Peruvian soda).

It is made using natural mineral water from the company's own source. According to the company's website, it is an excellent accompaniment to any type of food—including spicy food. This makes it the perfect beverage to go with the dishes of Arequipa.

#3: Arequipeña Beer

With the slogan "Arequipeña beer, made with pride", beer lovers should not miss tasting the strength and character of this beer.

Claire, a beer drinker, could not resist this pale lager. She found it a bit too hoppy, and didn't really enjoy its distinct taste—but keep in mind this is only one opinion, and it should not stop you from enjoying Arequipeña beer.

Spotlight

You feel the Arequipa pride at this restaurant. We were given Arequipa flags and enjoyed a wonderful discussion with the cook about the local Arequipa specialties. With a cozy environment, this is a true gem and an experience worth having in Lima.

Location: La Estrellita del Sur

Address: Esquina Jr. Pedro Conde y la Av. Ignacio Merino, Lince, Lima

Hours: Every day, 8:00 am – 7:00 pm

🍴 Piura Cuisine: Food and Drinks from the North of Peru

Piura, the largest city in Northern Peru, is known to be one of the best places to eat in the country. Founded in 1532, Piura is the oldest Spanish city in South America and is fondly referred to as *La Primera Ciudad* (the first city). Although Piura is not visited as often as Machu Picchu or the Amazon Jungle, it has a rich and interesting history.

The food from the area has been influenced by the important mestizo culture, with primary influences from the Spanish colonists, African slaves from Madagascar or Malagasy, and Chinese workers who migrated to work in the rice fields. This mestizo culture has created a very rich gastronomy.

To taste northern Peruvian cuisine without traveling to Piura, our friends Cecilia and Mae introduced us to Los Piuranos Restaurant: the best restaurant, in their opinion, serving traditional Piura food in Lima.

Los Piuranos Restaurant

At the restaurant, we sampled three typical dishes and one traditional drink from Piura.

#1: Tamalito Verde

Tamalito verde is a special kind of green tamale. Cornmeal is mixed with cilantro which gives it a nice, rich green color, and it's stuffed with onion and cheese. The tamales are cooked in banana leaves, but served without the leaves as a typical appetizer. Accompanying the *tamalito verde* is a delicious *huancaina* sauce made with yellow chili.

The consistency of the tamales is soft and melts in the mouth. The sweet and spice combination of the corn and chili is just perfect. Simply put, a delight!

#2: Seco de Chavelo: The Flagship Dish of Piura

The *seco de chavelo* is a typical dish of the lower Piura and is said to have been invented by a man named Chavelo more than 100 years ago. This dish combines seasoned, roasted plantains and pieces of beef with green peppers, onions, tomatoes, and *chicha* (fermented maize beer).

Seco de chavelo y carne seca

This dish reflects the diversity in Piura and is a fusion of tastes from Hispanics, Africans, and the indigenous people.

Rosemary absolutely fell in love with this dish. The sweet and salty combination of the plantains and beef was heavenly.

The texture was surprisingly soft and moist despite having the word *seco* (dry) in the description. This is a dish worthy of a trip to the north of Peru.

#3: Carne Seca

Carne seca are the thin strips of dried meat you see on the plate above. In Piura, we learned that it is customary to dry meat and share it amongst friends and family. This makes it a communal and celebratory dish that is well-loved.

Not having very many strips of meat on the plate, we jokingly had to fight to get enough. In a nutshell, we both loved this dish and would have liked to eat it as a full meal. That's always the challenge with little bites: you get just enough to tempt you, but not enough to fill you up.

Traditional Piurana Drinks

#1: Frozen Mango Ciruelo Juice

To accompany the meals and keep cool in the heat, the popular traditional drink in the region is mango ciruelo. This juice is made from a unique fruit that is found mainly in northern Peru. It is not grown on a large scale and therefore little known. It looks like a cross between a mango and a plum.

Though we didn't get to try the fruit, the frozen juice was quite a treat. The drink was a little heavy, but not too sweet. The best part is that it did not take away from the flavors of the food.

Northern Peruvian cuisine is often overlooked by visitors to the country who hit the high points of Lima and Cusco (for Machu Picchu). Even if your trip does not include a trip to the north of Peru, savor the delights of this unique cuisine from the oldest Spanish city of South America.

Spotlight

A very popular restaurant filled with locals. If you are planning to go on the weekend, it would be wise to make a reservation or dine outside of peak meal time hours. Enjoy amazing food and local drinks.

Location: **Los Piuranos**

Address: *Orquideas 2682, Lince 15046, Lima*

Hours: *Every day, 12:00 pm – 4:00 pm*

Amazon Cuisine: Food and Drinks from the Peruvian Amazon Jungle

As we continued to learn more about the rich and complex diversity of Peruvian cuisine, one of cuisines we were most excited to learn about and discover was food from the Peruvian Amazon Jungle.

While we didn't get a chance to physically visit the the Peruvian Amazon Jungle, we were delighted when our friends Cecilia and Mae recommended one of the most renowned restaurants in Lima that specializes in food from the Peruvian Amazon Jungle.

MEETING SULMA PENAHERRERA, CHEF AND OWNER OF EL BIJAO RESTAURANT, LIMA PERU

El Bijao restaurant is located on one of the busiest streets in the Lince neighborhood. We walked into this unassuming restaurant with green colored walls on a Thursday afternoon for lunch to taste the flavors of the Peruvian Amazon Jungle and meet the chef behind the food.

Chef and Owner Sulma Peñaherrera has been been serving dishes from the Peruvian Amazon Jungle for over 23 years. Sulma is from Iquitos, the largest city of the jungle, also known as the "Capital of the Peruvian Amazon." What's interesting to note is that Iquitos is the largest city in the world that is not accessible by road; visitors arrive by plane and boat only.

Rosemary and Claire with Sulma Penaherrera

Sulma was a wonderful host who took the time to share her story, from her humble beginnings to the success that she is today. As we talked, we noted several photos adorning the walls of her restaurant: one prominent picture was with Gastón Acurio, the famous Peruvian chef and ambassador of the Peruvian cuisine who has showcased Sulma's restaurant as one of the best places for Amazonian food in Peru.

The diversity of flora and fauna in the jungle offers a rich variety of food, all with unusual names and ingredients. The number of specialties and traditional dishes noted in the menu is considerable, and we were glad to have Sulma as our "translator" to help us understand the most typical dishes.

The main dishes from the Amazon include *paiche* (jungle fish), *tacacho con cecina* (pork raised in the jungle), *juane de gallina* (jungle chicken dishes) and more.

We learned that juices and liquors from Iquitos are very popular. We had the typical juices with our meal, and Sulma had us try a couple of the exotic Amazonian liquors, including the famous 7 Raices (seven roots), a liquor known for its aphrodisiac qualities.

#1: Juane: One of the Most Popular and Traditional Amazonian Dishes

Juane is one of the most traditional and popular dishes from the Peruvian Amazon Jungle. It is typically eaten on June 24th, when the residents of the Peruvian Amazon jungle celebrate the San Juan feast (Saint John the Baptist's Day). *Juane* is the dish eaten to celebrate this important Catholic festival, and it symbolizes the bridge between religion and the traditional way of life in the Amazon Jungle.

The typical preparation of *juane* is a bowl a bowl of rice filled with meat, boiled egg, black olives, and spices. All the ingredients are wrapped up in bijao leaves, which look like banana leaves, but come from palm trees that grow in the jungle. Everything is then cooked in clay pots and served in the bijao leaves.

#2: Juane de Pollo

El Bijao proposes a different menu every day. We went on a Thursday when *juane de pollo* (*juane* with chicken) was on the menu. It was served with plantains and a sauce made of chopped onions and cocona (a yellow fruit from the Amazon jungle). The dish was beautifully presented in a bijao leaf.

Juane de Gallina

As we dug into the rice, we uncovered chicken as well as an egg and olives. This dish is incredibly flavorful from the combination of poultry, olives and spices. The sauce spices it up a bit, and gives this enjoyable dish a very nice bite. This was one of our favorite dishes from the Amazon jungle and a classic dish you should not miss in Peru.

Traditional Drinks From the Peruvian Amazon Jungle

• Regional Drinks

The diversity of flavors in the Peruvian Amazon Jungle surprised and overwhelmed us. The combination of flavors and discovery of new textures in the food was like entering into a whole new culinary world.

This experience continued into the beverages. Exotic fruit juices and liquors are part of the culinary fabric. Juices accompany the meals, while liquors complete the experience and provide aphrodisiac or medicinal benefits.

This section puts a spotlight on some of the common local beverages found in the jungle. While there is much more diversity and breadth available, here are a couple of popular options to try.

• Fruit Juices from The Peruvian Amazon Jungle

#1: Cocona Juice

Local dishes from the Amazon are accompanied by juices made from the native fruits and plants. For example, *juane* is paired with cocona fruit juice. Cocona is a colorful fruit, about the size of a bell pepper. It is light yellow on the inside with edible seeds.

This favorite ingredient of the local gastronomy makes its way into spicy sauces, juices, nectars, ice creams, and even desserts.

As a juice, it is sweet and refreshing. Cocona is known to have important medicinal properties. It is rich in vitamins including iron and vitamin B5. It is said to help treat high blood pressure, diabetes and more. It is also used as a treatment for burns, and as a counter for venom.

#2: Camu Camu Juice

Camu camu berries grow wild on trees that grow along the rivers of the Amazon jungle. About the size of grapes, camu camu is known to be a fruit with one of the the highest levels of Vitamin C; it is reported to have up to 60 times more per serving than an orange. With the concentration of vitamins, it is said to be great for eye and gum health, it helps with the common cold, and it functions as an antioxidant.

It is not typically eaten as a fruit, but consumed widely as a fruit juice. It has tart sour taste, and is easy to drink.

#3: Aguajina Juice

The *aguaje* fruit is another nutrient-rich superfood known as the miracle fruit. It is packed with vitamins, proteins and oil, and it is consumed as a fruit juice.

Sulma described this as a "female-only juice." Apparently, *aguaje* fruit is used to improve women's health. This is due to its high phytoestrogen content. It is nicknamed the "curvy fruit" because it naturally increases female curves. It balances hormone levels during "that time of the month," eases hot flushes during menopause and is said to to even restore fertility.

Despite the many health benefits, we did not enjoy the taste of this juice. It was 'oily' and not very flavorful. It is drinkable, but not as easy to drink as the camu camu or cocona juices. However, it is a truly unique juice and one that any woman should not hesitate trying.

• Exotic Liquors

Liquors, we learned, are popular in the Peruvian Amazon jungle. Sulma told us that her hometown of Iquitos is famous for its liquors and beverages.

On display at the restaurant are a variety of strange-looking beverages. Many are infused with a variety of ingredients, from herbs to worms. Made with sugarcane alcohol, these beverages are known to have aphrodisiac properties.

The liquors have strange and provocative names. The most popular ones are: RC (Rompe Calzon, the "underpants breaker"), 7 Raices (Seven Roots), Chuchuhuasi, Uvachado, Levantate Lazaro (the Resurrection of Lazarus) and more.

At El Bijao, Sulma had us try three different kinds of regional drinks.

In three tiny glasses we tried 7 Raices (Seven Roots), uvachado (a liquor based on Amazonian black grapes and honey), and *coctél de cafe* (coffee cocktail).

We found the 7 Raices to be quite strong. The uvachado was our favorite: fruity, sweet and easy to drink. The *coctél de cafe* will definitely please any coffee drinker.

While discovering food from the Peruvian Amazon Jungle, be sure to complete the experience with the flavors of the juices and traditional liquors.

Spotlight

This is one of the best local restaurants for trying authentic food from the Amazon Jungle in Lima. Sulma will welcome you warmly and guide you through the unique menu. Be sure to sample the local juices and liquors.

Location: El Bijao *(www.facebook.com/elbijaolima)*

Address: *Av. Ignacio Merino 2051 Lince, Lima*

Hours: *Sunday to Thursday, 11:00 am – 6:00 pm; Friday and Saturday, 11:00 am – 9:00 pm*

DISCOVERING AMAZON FUSION FOOD AT TK RESTAURANT

One evening when walking around the Lince *barrio* (neighborhood) where we stayed at an Airbnb, we stumbled upon TK Restaurant.

Having just eaten the traditional Amazon dishes at El Bijao, we looked at the menu from the outside and were surprised, because none of the dishes advertised looked similar to what we had just eaten.

A young man came outside to gently greet us and took the time to explain the menu and the different dishes. Intrigued, we took a table by the entrance with a clear view of the kitchen.

Surprisingly delicious Amazon fusion dish

Much to our surprise, when the young man came back with a complimentary appetizer, he introduced himself as the chef and owner of the restaurant. He name is Ivan and he told us he had just opened his restaurant one month ago. Before that, he had a stand at the local market where he was selling traditional food from the Amazon. But when he opened his restaurant, he decided to focus on Amazon fusion food and offer Peruvian "fast food" with an Amazonian flair.

With his recommendation, we ordered two dishes. One was a typical dish from the Amazon Jungle, and the second was a fusion of Amazon and Peruvian flavors.

#1: Tacacho Con Cecina

Tacacho con cecina is a typical dish from the Amazon Rainforest of Peru. When we ordered this meal, we didn't know what to expect. Visually, the dish was incredibly surprising. On the plate were two round balls and thinly cut slices of dried, smoked pork.

At first glance, the dish looked very dry. However, after the taking the first bite, it was surprisingly moist. Ivan told us the round balls are made of mashed up bananas. At his restaurant, instead of using green bananas which is typical, he mixes green and yellow bananas to give the balls their unique taste. The *cecina* is dried, smoked pork made with traditional spices from the jungle, which gives it a distinctive flavor.

Putting the appearance aside, the meal was quite moist and very well seasoned. The banana balls had an interesting salty and sweet flavor, and the *cecina* was out of this world! Succulent and savory, this was a simple and tasty dish.

#2: TK Chaufa Mix

Venturing into the fusion space, we ordered the TK Chaufa Mix. The main ingredients in this dish are *arroz chaufa and cecina* accompanied by fried plantains. What makes this dish a true fusion is the use of *arroz chaufa,* which is very a popular Peruvian-Chinese fried rice (see the **Chifa** section).

Pairing it with Amazon-style *cecina* (pork) and blending the tastes of *chifa* and the jungle made it truly unique. Ivan told us his goal was to introduce Amazonian food to the locals by using popular fast food dishes with an Amazon twist.

The Chaufa Mix was absolutely excellent. The rice was full of flavor and the chopped up pieces of the *cecina* enhanced the flavors. Like the *tacacho* dish, the *cecina* was moist, tender and delicious: a really unique combination. Most of the typical fast food like *arroz chaufa* dishes are made with chicken, so using the *cecina* instead makes this dish really stand out. This is a delicious way to ease oneself into Amazonian food.

With chef, owner Ivan

Spotlight

A casual spot and a great place to sample a twist on food from the Amazon Jungle. Let Ivan walk you through the menu and make recommendations for which dishes to try.

Location: **TK Restaurant** *(www.facebook.com/TkRestaurantOficial)*

Address: *Jr. Soledad 516, Lince, Lima*

Hours: *Every day, 11:00 am – 7:00 pm*

LIMA, PERU

Lima: The Gastronomy Capital of South America

Exterior of the Presidential Palace, Lima

Peru's thriving culinary scene is the byproduct of a period of prosperity that began about 10 years ago, following decades of economic crisis and civil war. Food has become the glue that has held together a nation that experienced difficult times over the last forty years. Today, Peru's importance as a culinary destination rivals that of France.

Peruvians identify with their cuisine like other Latin American countries do with sports or music. It is the main source of national pride. When we first arrived in Lima and told our taxi driver we were visiting the capital to eat, he immediately swelled up with pride and rattled off names and addresses of restaurants we should not miss.

Lima is the best place to taste the diversity of Peruvian cuisine. The city is huge and spread out over 43 different *distritos* (districts). It is a city with rich colonial architecture and an incredible waterfront with gorgeous sunsets along the Pacific Ocean.

The historic city center of Lima is the colonial capital of Peru, founded by Spanish conquistador Francisco Pizarro in 1535. The historical center was declared a World Heritage Site by UNESCO in 1988 and and a "Cultural Patrimony of Humanity" in 1996.

Lima Cuisine

If you can't make it to every region of Peru, a tour through Lima alone will allow you to sample cuisines from every corner of the country, as we saw in the previous sections: each of those regional dishes was found in Lima.

That said, Lima also has specialties that are unique to the city. *Ceviche* is said to be the most fresh in Lima due to its proximity to the ocean. Other specialties like *pollo a brasa* (rotisserie chicken), *causa limeña* (a layered potato dish) and desserts like *suspiro a la limeña* (a custard referred to as the "Sigh of Lima") are reputed to have gotten their start here. Inca Kola, Peru's national soft drink, also began in Lima. This section goes into more detail about these specialties.

A Note About the Districts in Lima

Lima often gets a bad reputation for its chaotic traffic and disorienting urban sprawl. While this was not our experience in Lima, this was the message we heard before arriving in the capital.

As a result, visitors are often directed to the main tourist district of Miraflores. This trendy neighborhood has a stunning boardwalk filled with the types of restaurants and shopping malls one would find at any major city around the world. The area is also controlled by special police for visitors and tourists, which gives it a highly sanitized atmosphere.

Many of the top gastronomy restaurants in Lima are located around Miraflores or within a short cab ride.

On our hunt for the local and authentic flavors of Peru, we deliberately stayed away from the Miraflores neighborhood. Instead, we based ourselves in a local working class district named Lince.

Staying with locals via Airbnb, we later discovered that Lince is renowned for street foods, speciality foods and a plethora of local food markets.

While many of the traditional dishes and drinks are available at the upscale restaurants in Miraflores, we are featuring them from where the vast majority of *los limeños* (people from Lima) eat and enjoy them.

To explore Peru like a local, we encourage you to visit and eat at the local farmers' markets. Get in line with the locals and queue up for popular street foods and desserts. Try new foods at the local festivals. In the next section, we'll show you how to go deeper and embrace the culture through unique Peruvian specialties.

Authentic Specialties Not to Miss in Lima
#1 Aji de Gallina
#2 Arroz con Pollo
#3 Causa
#4 Ceviche
#5 Lomo Saltado
#6 Papa a la Huancaína
#7 Pollo a la Brasa
#8 Tacu Tacu

Street Foods
#1: Anticuchos
#2: Rachi
#3: Peruvian Sandwiches and Butifarra
#4: Peruvian Tamales

Desserts
#1: Arroz con Leche and Mazamorra Morada
#2: Picarones
#3: Suspiro a la Limeña
#4: Turrón de Doña Pepa

Beverages
#1: Pisco Sour
#2: Chilcano
#3: Inca Kola
#4: Cusqueña Beer
#5: Peruvian Fresh Juices and "Jugo Especial"

Unique Peruvian Local Fruits
#1: Lúcuma
#2: Pitahaya
#3: Pacay
#4: Cocona
#5: Camu Camu
#6: Maracuya
#7: Tumbo
#8: Aguaje
#9: Mamey Sapote
#10: Noni

Local Markets
#1: Mercado de Surquillo #1
#2: Mercado de Surquillo #2
#3: Mercado Central
#4: Terminal Pesquero

Authentic Specialties Not to Miss in Lima

#1: Ají de Gallina
From the Sierra, available everywhere

The most striking thing about this dish is its bright yellow color, which comes from the *ají amarillo* (yellow chili) in its sauce.

A fusion of Spanish and Quechua ingredients, this dish begins with a thick cream made up of yellow chili, breadcrumbs, egg, parmesan cheese, pecans, milk, onion and garlic. The *ají* is one of the most popular spices that is used to add extra flavor in meals.

Succulent chicken is cooked in this delicious creamy, mildly spicy sauce, and served with rice and/or yellow boiled potatoes. A wonderfully delicious comfort food, *ají de gallina* is popular in the rainy season.

Ají de Gallina

#2: Arroz con Pollo
From the Sierra, available everywhere

When our Airbnb host Patricia decided to make us dinner one evening, she chose to make her all-time favorite childhood dish: *arroz con pollo* (rice with chicken).

We got back to the apartment after Patricia had started cooking and were surprised to see her standing over her blender with a green mixture spinning at high speeds.

Arroz con Pollo (Photo credit: Marlon E)

We had never seen rice and chicken prepared in this manner. It was cilantro, she told us, as we waited eagerly with anticipation.

Patricia prepared the chicken with peas, carrots, red pepper, tomatoes, onion and cilantro-infused rice. The *arroz con pollo* was served with a side of potatoes.

Every country in Latin America has its own take on this meal. A liberal dose of cilantro colors this dish bright green in the traditional version, but we learned there are variations in many different colors, depending on the region. This dish can be red with *ají panca* pepper, yellow from saffron native to north Peru, or almost white.

This signature dish is a popular mainstay in the national cuisine. Don't skip this seemingly familiar dish while in Peru—the bright colors and flavors will not disappoint.

PERUVIAN ARROZ CON POLLO RECIPE
Courtesy of: Comidas Peruanas [1]

Preparation Time: 15 minutes
Cooking Time: 30 minutes
Total: 45 minutes
Serves: 8 people

Ingredients:
- 1 onion, chopped in very small squares
- 1 bell pepper julienned
- 1 1/2 tablespoons yellow pepper
- 1 tablespoon red pepper
- 1 1/2 tablespoons ground garlic
- 1/2 cup vegetable oil
- 1/2 cup of peas
- 2 carrots, chopped in small squares
- 1 cup of Cusco beer (optional)
- 8 pieces of chicken
- 1 1/2 cups cilantro
- 4 cups white rice
- 1 cube of chicken broth (Knorr or Maggi for example)
- Cumin, salt and pepper to taste

Cooking Instructions:
1. Season chicken pieces with salt, pepper and cumin before frying. Mix well so both seasonings are in all parts of the chicken.
2. Put the oil in a pot and when it is hot add the chicken pieces.
3. Fry them a little until they are a little golden but not completely. Remove and put them in a covered container so they do not cool
4. While the chicken is frying, liquefy the cilantro. Blend the cilantro leaves with a little chicken broth and a little bit of beer (not too much liquid). You can use water as a substitute for the broth.
5. Remove the chicken pieces, and in the same pot add the onion, garlic, yellow pepper, red pepper, salt, and pepper. And the cube of chicken broth. Fry everything for a couple of minutes until the onion is golden, stirring often so that it does not burn.
6. After a minute or so, add the chicken pieces to finish frying them along, with all the cilantro dressing and the a cup of beer. (The rest is for you.)

1 http://comidasperuanas.net/arroz-con-pollo-peruano/

7. Wait a minute and add 3 cups of water (making 4 cups of liquid, including beer) and wait for it to finish cooking the chicken completely.
8. Once the chicken is cooked, remove the pieces and place them in covered container so they do not cool. Add 3 more cups water, chopped carrots, peas and rice. In total there should be 7 cups of liquid (water and beer) for 4 cups of rice. Adjust seasonings to taste.
9. Stir from time to time so the rice does not stick to the bottom. When you have reduced the liquid, lower the temperature to simmer for about 20 minutes.
10. In the last 5 minutes before the rice is done, place the pieces of chicken and the julienned pepper on top and re-cover the pot.
11. Wait until the time is up, and enjoy!

#3: Causa

From the Sierra (or Costa), available everywhere

Causa is a traditional dish deeply tied to the history of Peru, though its origins are a matter of debate and legend. The name *causa* comes from a Quechua word meaning "sustenance of life". Back in the Inca period, this dish was originally a simple layering of two native Andean ingredients, potatoes and *ají* pepper.

Another story from its history says that during the war for independence, the liberator José de San Martín walked into a restaurant where there was almost no food. The cook mashed some potatoes, put some meat and vegetables in the middle, and gave it to the liberator. When the liberator asked the name of the dish, the cook answered, "it's for the cause" (meaning the cause the independence). Local women at the time are also said to have stuffed potatoes with protein during war, also for the cause.

While the stories and the recipes may vary, the featured ingredient of this dish is the potato, mashed together with ground yellow *ají* pepper and lemon. The potatoes are then stuffed with chicken, tuna or other variations—it's always delicious.

The two most typical presentations are *causa limeña* and *causa rellena*.

Causa limeña is layered with potato, tuna, avocado and tomato.

In *causa rellena*, the potatoes are stuffed with shredded chicken breast and tomatoes.

Causa Limeña

Whether we ate it on the streets or in restaurants, *limeña* or *rellena* style, we always enjoyed the delicious simplicity of this dish and its rich heritage.

Causa Rellena

> ## Spotlight
> To taste this meal in all its variations, visit *Mi Causa*, where you can find 38 different varieties!
>
> **Location:** *Mi Causa*
>
> **Address:** *Avenida La Mar 814, Miraflores*
>
> **Hours:** *Tuesday to Sunday, 12:30pm – 5:30pm*

#4: Ceviche
From the Costa, available everywhere

Ceviche is so beloved that it is considered both Lima's "dish of the city" as well as Peru's favorite dish. The Peruvian government created National Ceviche Day in 2008 to honor *ceviche* as part of Peru's national heritage. It is celebrated every year on June 28th.

The history of *ceviche* usually invokes a spirited discussion. The birthplace of *ceviche* is disputed between Peru and Ecuador, two countries with amazing varieties of fish and shellfish. The dish is also often credited to the ancient Inca civilizations. One Inca emperor is said to have enjoyed his fresh fish marinated in *tumbo* fruit (see **Unique Local Fruits** in Lima section for more about the fruit) and required it be delivered to him high in Cusco, capital of the Inca Empire.

The account we heard most often was that *ceviche* evolved from a dish that was brought to Peru by Moorish women accompanying Spanish conquistadors.

Regardless of the theories surrounding the origins of the dish, in Peru *ceviche* is revered. Everyone wants to claim its origin story.

Ceviche is essentially a raw dish that consists of fish soaked in citrus juices (such as lime) with spiced with chili peppers. There are just 5 ingredients in the national dish of Peru: raw fish, salt red onions and *ají*, Peru's unique line of chili peppers, all doused in lime juice.

The acidic marinade, called *leche de tigre* (tiger's milk), 'cooks' the fish and changes the proteins in the fish, making it firm and opaque. *Ceviche* is often accompanied by *camote* (sweet potatoes) and *choclo* (large, white Andean corn), which are both native to Peru.

Freshly prepared ceviche

TIPS TO KEEP IN MIND

- *Ceviche* is traditionally eaten at lunch, when the fish is most fresh.
- *Ceviche* is typically prepared in two traditional styles, *pescado* and *mixto*. The *pescado* is the traditional mix of thinly cut slices of fish, while the *mixto* adds squid, octopus and scallops.
- *Ceviche* is typically eaten at *cevicherías* (restaurants that specialize in *ceviche*). In Lima alone, there are more than 20,000 *cevicherías* to keep you busy.
- Don't be surprised by the number of people eating *ceviche* for lunch. *Limeños* (people of Lima) are crazy about *ceviche*. In Peru as a whole, people eat an average of **44 pounds of fish every year, compared to just 16 pounds in the U.S.**[2]

DISCOVERING CEVICHE IN LIMA

Knowing where to find good *ceviche* in Lima can be a daunting task, especially when seeking a local experience. After asking to our friends and hosts where locals go for good *ceviche*, we were advised to try it at the four different kinds of eateries: restaurants, *huariques*, *mercados* and street vendors.

"*Wow*", is what we said every single time we tried *ceviche* at the various eateries. We were blown away by the quality of the fish and the combinations of flavors. It didn't matter if we were at a restaurant or at the local market; the fish and seafood was incredibly fresh and it was some of the most delicious seafood we've ever tasted.

The onions, limes and spices give it a tangy bite, and then the unique sweet taste of the *camote* comes into play. The sublime mix of flavors is simply incredible. It's understandable why this dish has it's own national day.

While in Lima, experience *ceviche* at the different kinds of eateries. Go beyond the popular restaurants in tourist destinations. Pull up a stool at a *huarique* or local market to experience their unique take on this specialty.

Below are some of the our favorite local eateries for *ceviche* in Lima:

Restaurants

- **El Mordisco** is a local popular restaurant in the Lince district, with amazing *ceviche*. Av. Petit Thouars 2631, Lince, Lima. (www.facebook.com/El-Mordisco)

2 https://www.st.nmfs.noaa.gov/st1/fus/fus04/08_perita2004.pdf

Huariques

For a local family-style experience, Punto Azul has six locations in Lima. The one below (our favorite) is the original location.
- **Punto Azul**, Esq. Javier Prado con Petit Thouars, San Isidro, Lima. (www.puntoazulrestaurante.com)

Lining up at lunch time for fresh ceviche at the outdoor Punto Azul restaurant

Local Markets

You'll find ceviche at most local local markets. In addition to the two main markets listed below, we also enjoyed it at the neighborhood market in the Lince district.
- Mercado de Surquillo, Paseo de la Republica, block 53, Surquillo, Lima.
- Mercado Central, corner of Ayacucho & Ucayali, Lima Centro, Lima.

#5: Lomo Saltado
From the Sierra, available everywhere

> *"The lomo saltado is one of the dishes that brings together flavor, ingredients, fusion and cooking techniques. While it's not a native dish, it is a dish that I can recommend to foreigners, because its flavors are universal."*
>
> **– Cecilia Portella Morote**

Though *lomo saltado* is considered a traditional Peruvian dish today, it is actually a fusion of Chinese and Peruvian foods called c*hifa* (see the **Chifa** section).

The mix of influences is immediately evident in the ingredients: strips of beef, onions, tomatoes and *ají amarillo* chili are stir-fried together with soy sauce, garlic and cilantro. The dish is served Chinese-style with rice and the surprising addition of french fries (using Peruvian potatoes).

Lomo Saltado

On your trip to Peru, you will find *lomo saltado* everywhere. We had the opportunity to eat this classic dish at local markets as well as at *chifa* restaurants.

This flavorful and absolutely delicious dish is not to be missed. This dish perfectly blends the tastes and aromas of Peruvian and Chinese ingredients together.

As our friend Cecilia Portella Morote would say, "its flavors are universal."

#6: Papa a la Huancaína
from the Andes, available everywhere
Papa a la Huancaína is quintessentially Peruvian and undoubtedly Andean: its name translates to "Potatoes of the Lady from Huancayo." This classic Peruvian dish is technically an appetizer, but can be eaten anytime. Pronounced *papa-a-la-wan-cayina*, it was invented accidentally more than a century ago.

Story has it that it was created by a poor farming woman from Huancayo, the capital of the Junin region in the central highlands of Peru. She created it to compliment the potatoes she was selling to the miners and railway workers working on Peru's Central Railway tracks from Huancayo to Lima.

Papa a la Huancaína

Today, the Ferrovias Central Railway line boasts the second-highest tracks in the world, topping out at 15,689 feet above sea level. Apparently, the dish became so popular that it was the commemorative dish of the railway's opening.

The dish consists of sliced boiled potatoes, ideally from Huancayo, served in a spicy creamy sauce called *Huancaína*. The sauce uses the iconic *ají amarillo* pepper, made into a paste and mixed with fresh cheese, oil, salt, pepper, and evaporated milk. The sauced potatoes are garnished with hard-boiled eggs and black olives.

The taste of this dish spans a spectrum of flavors, ranging from cheesy and spicy to starchy and slightly bitter.

The dish made history again in 2008, when the largest serving of *Papa a la Huancaina* was made in Huancayo. A very long table was installed on a city street, and 1500 kilograms of potatoes, eggs and olives were used to serve 12,000 plates of the dish. (The event was recorded in the Guinness Book of World Records when it beat the previous record of a mere 8,000 plates.)

#7: Pollo a la Brasa

This Peruvian-style roast chicken is so delicious and popular that the Peru National Institute of Culture declared *pollo a brasa* a "National Culinary Speciality" in 2004.

And as Peru knows how to celebrate its gastronomy, *pollo a la brasa* has its own national holiday on the third Sunday of July.

This dish is known as "Peruvian-style chicken", charcoal chicken", or "rotisserie chicken", and it is one of the most popular and most consumed dishes in Peru.

This Peruvian fast food was developed in 1950 by Roger Schuler, a Swiss resident who was living in Peru. His chicken farm near Lima went bankrupt, and to make ends meet and support his family, he started selling whole roasted chickens with the slogan, "*Eat as much chicken over coals as you can for only five Soles.*"

His tasty chickens and inexpensive prices became so popular that he needed to cook the chickens faster. He contacted Franz Ulrich, a Swiss friend who owned a metal mechanics shop, and asked him to develop a device to cook several chickens at once.

Thus, the *rotombo* oven, or *speido*, was invented. With 6 metal rods that can each hold 8 baby chickens, this method can hold 40 to 50 chickens at once. The metal rods spin clockwise and independently at very high temperatures (300-370 degrees F), cooking the chickens uniformly

while keeping the juices and flavors intact.

In the 1950's Roger and Franz teamed up to open the first *pollo a la brasa* restaurant in Lima, called La Granja Azul. Seeing their success, many other *pollerías* started opening all over the city. Today, La Granja Azul remains popular and you cannot miss the *pollerías*, as they are on every corner.

Rotombo (speido) oven at Las Canastas, Lima

The secret of the success of Pollo a la Brasa resides in its cooking method and marinades. Each *pollería* as its own secret marinade recipe, and a rotisserie over wood coals to give the chicken a sublime smoky flavor.

The original recipe from La Granja Azul calls for the chicken to be seasoned with salt and cooked over carob tree firewood for the best flavors.

A POLLO A LA BRASA EXPERIENCE AT LAS CANASTAS

To try *pollo a la brasa*, we asked gastronomy critic Cecilia and her friend Mae to take us to a restaurant of their choice for the most authentic and typical dish. It was between Pardos Chicken and Las Canastas; they chose to take us to Las Canastas, which they said "had bigger chickens" than Pardos.

Walking into Las Canastas is not like walking into a typical fast food joint. The particular restaurant we went to in the neighborhood or *barrio* de Miraflores was a large restaurant with seating for about 60-100 people.

The menu was surprisingly short. They offered a quarter chicken for about USD $5, half of a chicken for about USD $9, and about USD $14 for a whole chicken. We ordered one full chicken to be split 4 ways (*cuarto,* one fourth), with the typical sides of *papas fritas* (potatoes) and salads.

Part of the appeal of eating at a *polleria* is that they are not fancy, and eating the chicken with your hands is encouraged. In a typical Peruvian fashion, we started the meal with pisco sours while waiting for our chicken.

Eating *pollo a la brasa* is not like eating any good ol' chicken. There is a protocol that must be followed around this Peruvian fast food. To drink, you start out with the pisco sour as we did. While eating the meal, one can choose to drink either Inca Kola or *chicha morada* (see the **Beverages** of Cusco section).

We would have to say that this is one of the most delicious chickens we have ever eaten. The herbs and spices coated the skin and made it beautifully crisp as well. The chicken was rich with flavor and as juicy as you can imagine.

Rosemary had the *pecho* (chicken breast), which can sometimes be dry. She was delighted to find the breast savory and well spiced. Claire had the *pierna* (chicken leg), which was fragrant and so succulent that the chicken meat was practically falling off the bone.

With the high quality of taste and flavors, you could tell that the chickens were raised humanely in low-stress environments.

Pollo a la brasa is not just "chicken" in Peru; originally, *pollo a la brasa* was for Peruvians of high socioeconomic status. It wasn't until sometime in the 1970s that the consumption came to include Peruvians of middle and lower socioeconomic status. Today, *pollo a la brasa* is Peruvian fast food that is now accessible and eaten by all.

If your travels take you to Peru, be sure to eat *pollo a la brasa*. By doing so, you will not only enjoy the delicious chicken but also participate in a piece of Peruvian culture that was once reserved for the privileged few.

Location: Las Canastas *(www.lascanastas.com)*

Address: *Av. Angamos Oeste 599, Miraflores, Lima*

Hours: *Every day, 11:00 am – 11:00 pm*

#8: Tacu Tacu
From the Sierra (or Costa), available everywhere

Tacu tacu is a typical Peruvian dish whose heritage is from the Afro-Peruvian community. Its origins are humble. Some say that it was first cooked by African slaves brought by the Spanish conquistadors to the south of Lima.

Transformed by African hands, this dish was a simple way to use up leftover rice and beans into a savory combination. Leftover rice and beans would be mashed together, fried and molded into a gigantic tamale-like shape. It is often served with a cheap cut of beef and a fried egg on top. The key to a great *tacu tacu* is making sure the exterior is toasty and golden with a slight crunchiness and a tender interior.

Seafood Tacu Tacu

Today, you will find many variations of *tacu tacu*. Some cooks will use different kinds of beans and a variety of vegetables like asparagus and leeks. Others will replace the beef with seafood. Despite these variations, there is one consistent step: the rice and beans are typically prepared the day before.

We tried *tacu tacu* at Lobo de Mar Cebicheria in the Miraflores district, and we were pleasantly delighted. This particular version was prepared with seafood (*tacu tacu mariscos*) and it was fresh and flavorful. The portion was humongous and designed to be shared: a perfect way to discover this Afro-Peruvian treat.

TACU TACU AT CEVICHERIA LOBO DE MAR

If you go to Cevicheria Lobo de Mar, you won't find *tacu tacu* on the menu. Like many *criollo* (homemade) dishes, *tacu tacu* is not standard restaurant fare. For our first experience with this dish, we were lucky to be with Deborah, our Spanish teacher from Chicago, who was visiting family in Lima.

She took us to her favorite restaurant in the Miraflores district, and though it wasn't in their standard offerings, she asked the owner/chef to prepare it for us. He happily obliged, and we learned a valuable lesson: for some *criollo* dishes, if you ask nicely and are very lucky, you'll be served a heaping meal of a unique dish.

Lobo de Mar is a *cevichería*, which means that fish and seafood dishes feature prominently. We started out with a plate of *ceviche pescado* and followed this up with *tacu tacu mariscos*. The chef surprised us with another plate of lightly fried shrimp and seafood, which was also off the menu.

This *tacu tacu* dish was unusual in presentation, but packed with flavor. Stuffed in a crescent-shaped pocket of rice were delicious prawns, octopus and different kinds of fish, all sitting in a delightful dark sauce.

This is a meal you want to have when you are hungry or prepared to share. Inventive stuffings range from seafood to creative uses of leftovers. While you may not find this dish easily, it is worth seeking out.

Rosemary and Claire with the chef at Lobo de Mar

Location: *Cevicheria Lobo de Mar*
Address: *Colon 587 (Juan Fanning), Miraflores, Lima*
Hours: *Tuesday to Sunday, 10:30 am – 5:00 pm*

Street Food

We never miss out on street food in our quest for authentic dining, and of all the South American countries we visited—from Argentina to Uruguay to Chile—Peru had the strongest showing of street food culture.

On the avenues of Lima, it's possible to observe a rotating selection of vendors at all different times of day. In the morning, street carts sell breakfast foods; they're replaced with beverage carts in the afternoon, and completely different carts emerge at dusk with popular night-time favorites.

While we couldn't taste every possible offering, below are the highlights of typical and traditional favorites that you can find on the streets.

#1: Anticuchos

Anticuchos are probably one of the most traditional street foods you will see in Peru. As the Spanish name suggests, this is literally meat on a stick served with a boiled potato skewered on the end.

The most traditional *anticuchos* are *anticuchos de corazón*: grilled beef hearts. Tipped as usual with a boiled potato, these are served with *ají* chili sauce.

Watching the preparation of the *anticuchos* is fascinating; all the skewers are lined up at once and filled with pieces of cow heart, beef, or chicken. They are grilled for five to seven minutes and basted regularly with sauce. The first bite of *anticuchos de corazón* is surprising: it has a hearty beef flavor, but a different texture; the heart meat feels slippery, tender, and chewy. We enjoyed them so much that we had to have them a second time.

Beef hearts on skewers waiting to be cooked

The story of *anticuchos* is very much part of the national story of Peru, dating back to the arrival of African slaves in the 16th century. From time to time, the Spanish colonialists would slaughter cows for food, and they would give the innards—which they considered garbage—to their slaves. The African slaves seasoned the pieces with ingredients from the Andes and Spain, transforming them into delicious morsels of meat.

The story goes that after the slaves were freed in 1874, they moved to the cities to start their new lives. Poor, hungry, and in search for work, mothers started selling *anticuchos* at neighborhood corners. The delicious smells of spiced, grilled meat attracted the resident *Limeños*, who would stop and enjoy them, quickly making them a daily habit. The number of *anticucheras* quickly grew and spread throughout Lima and other cities.

Today, *anticuchos* are loved and eaten by all: young, old, rich and poor. They are a part of the traditional Peruvian cuisine, and a hallmark food during the July celebration of *Fiestas Patrias* (Independence day).

Spotlight

A very local experience of eating on the street, you'll see long lines of people waiting to bite into this sumptuous delight. Take your place in line and order like the locals. You'll find street vendors everywhere, but we particularly liked Dona Pochita.

Location: Anticuchos Dona Pochita

Address: Av. Ignacio Merino 2316, Lince

Hours: Everyday except Sunday, open from 5:30 pm – 12:00 am

#2: Rachi

You'll often see *rachi* sold on street carts alongside *anticuchos*. While not as delicious as *anticuchos*, *rachi* is no less important in Peruvian cuisine. Typically served in the Andes and popular throughout Peru, *rachi* is essentially seasoned cow's belly served on a stick, served with garlic, Peruvian corn, salt and pepper.

We'll be frank: we didn't enjoy *rachi*. We found the texture too chewy, and the flavor was not as delicious as the *anticuchos*. Still, it's a dish well worth trying to eat as the locals do.

> ### Spotlight
> On the grill next to *anticuchos*, you will see skewers of *rachi*. Feel free to grab a stick and try this other popular street food.
>
> **Location:** Anticuchos Dona Pochita
>
> **Address:** Av. Ignacio Merino 2316, Lince
>
> **Hours:** Everyday except Sunday, open from 5:30 pm – 12:00 am

#3: Peruvian Sandwiches and Butifarra

As dusk turns to night in Lima, mobile carts turn up along the streets with all different types of sandwiches on offer. From 7pm to 8pm, vendors offer hamburgers, chicken sandwiches and the famous pork sandwich *butifarra*.

If you want to try Peruvian sandwiches, don't hesitate to sample what the sandwich carts have available. We tried two different kinds: the local speciality *butifarra*, as well as a hamburger sandwich.

The clear winner was the *butifarra*, also called *jamón del país* (country ham). Crusty French-style bread is piled with slices of pork, onion, *palta* (avocado), and *ají* pepper to give this delicious sandwich a slight spicy kick.

The hamburger sandwich was much less impressive, and nothing like the juicy and succulent hamburgers you may find in the U.S. The beef patty, onions, tomato slices and buns may all be familiar, but a *picante* sauce gives the Peruvian burger a nice bite.

If you are craving Peruvian street food and want to try a Peruvian sandwich, go with the *butifarra*.

#4: Peruvian Tamales

Tamales are a staple found across South America in a wide array of flavors and ingredients. In Peru, the tamales are made with Peruvian white or yellow corn. Cornmeal dough is filled with meat (usually chicken or pork), boiled eggs, olives, nuts, and *ají* pepper. They're topped with red onion, steamed, and wrapped in a banana leaf. This makes for an ideal snack on the go.

Peruvian tamales

One of the best places to try tamales is on the streets where the vendors are making them to order, or while visiting Mercado Surquillo #1, one of the most important farmers' markets in Lima.

Unwrap the banana leaves and enjoy the tasty combination of the mild sweet corn meal with the spicy bites of meat. These are a great option while strolling the streets of Lima.

Desserts

#1: Arroz con Leche & Mazamorra Morada

Street vendors serve two classic Peruvian desserts, *arroz con leche* and *mazamorra morada,* from big pots on their mobile carts.

Arroz con leche is the Peruvian version of rice pudding, brought to Peru by the Spanish. It is a simple dessert made with rice, sweetened condensed milk and evaporated milk.

Mazamorra morada is a traditional and popular dessert made from purple corn, fruit and *harina de camote* (sweet potato starch).

These desserts can be eaten in three ways. You can have the *arroz con leche* by itself. You can eat like a *limeña* and have the *mazamorra morada* by itself. Or, you can have it as a "classical", which means equal servings of both the *arroz con leche* and *mazamorra morada*.

Classical version with both arroz con leche & mazamorra morada

We tried the classical dessert to get the best of both worlds. We had both sampled *arroz con leche* before, and found the Peruvian version to be too sweet and thick. After a few bites, we both much preferred the *mazamorra morada*. However, given their popularity in Peru, both are worth trying out on your next trip.

Spotlight

Anywhere where there is street food, you'll likely find a street vendor selling *arroz con leche* and *mazamorra morada*. Get a "classical" so you can try both desserts in one serving.

#2: Picarones

Even though *picarones* look like a kind of doughnut, they are actually quite different and unique to Peru. The principal ingredients are sweet potato and squash. They are deep fried and served with cane syrup

Picarones

called *chancaca*. It's traditional to serve *picarones* when eating *anticuchos*.

The *picarones* are typically served in sets of four. The first time we got our order, we were surprised and thought we would not finish them; it was after a big meal and we were already stuffed. After the first couple of bites, we understood clearly why these little fried fritters were so popular. The combination of sweet potato and squash is heavenly, and not overly sweet. No questions asked: these should be on your list to sample.

Spotlight

At most local restaurants, markets or events, *picarones* will be one of the desserts served. Keep an eye out for them and make room for these delicious bites.

#3: Suspiro a la Limeña

Suspiro a la limeña is Lima's most popular *criollo* dessert. The bottom layer of the dessert is based on *manjar blanco*, the Peruvian equivalent for what is known as *dulce de leche* elsewhere in South America. It is topped with a smooth meringue cloud spiked with Port wine and a touch of cinnamon.

Suspiro de limeña at local festival

This dessert was first known as the "Royal Delight of Peru," but it was renamed by Peruvian poet and writer José Gálvez who called it "a woman's sigh".

We tried this dessert at a gastronomy festival in Lima. While it has a rich heritage, we quickly discovered why it was served in a small portion. This dessert is extremely rich, and it's a good idea to take small bites and keep sighs of contentment from becoming sighs of overindulgence.

This classic dessert has much history and flavor. Beloved across the country, it is worth indulging in this classic Lima dessert!

#4: Turrón de Doña Pepa

This traditional dessert of Lima is linked to the religious activities of *Señor de los Milagros* (Lord of Miracles) that takes place every October. Legend has it that this dessert's invention was a miraculous one.

The Procession of the Lord of Miracles is an important religious Catholic festival in Peru. It pays homage to an image of Christ believed to have miraculous powers.

According to religious history, the image was painted on a wall by a West African slave in the Las Nazarenas Church in the district of Pachacamilla, which is now downtown Lima.

In 1655, a massive earthquake struck Lima, reducing much of the city to dust. Miraculously, the only thing left standing was the wall where a few years earlier the Angolan slave had painted the Christ image.

In 1687 another earthquake hit Lima. Once again, much of the city was destroyed, except the wall with the image.

People began to worship the image and came from across the country to see it. It was a common belief that the image gave protection from earthquakes and could even cure people of illnesses.

In the 19th century, one of the people that came to see the image was Josefa Maraminillo, an Afro-Peruvian slave known as Doña Pepa. She suffered badly from paralysis and ventured to Lima to pray to El Señor de los Milagros and ask him to cure her.

Soon after, she felt better and no longer suffered any pain.

Eternally grateful, Doña Pepa wanted to give back somehow. It is said that in a dream, saints appeared to her and gave her the recipe for a dessert. The next day, she walked through the crowds at Las Nazarenas and began to hand out the god-given recipe, a sort of layered anise flavored nougat drizzled with *chancaca* syrup and topped with sprinkles and candy.

Every October thereafter, she would come to Lima and distribute her sweets, which became known as *Turrón de Doña Pepa*.

While they are popular in October, you will find them available all year round. Sweet tooths will love this extremely sweet and sticky delight. You'll find many *turrón* varieties in Lima. Some nougat treats are softer than others, some dissolve in your mouth, and others are much drier.

Turrones from local store Turrones San Jose, Lima

Location: Turrones San Jose

Address: Av. Ignacio Merino, Lince 15046

Beverages

Your visit to Peru will no doubt introduce you a variety of local Peruvian beverages with wildly diverse flavors: sweet, sour, fermented options and more. While you already know Peru has exquisite gastronomy, the local beverages are also monuments of domestic pride and symbols of Peruvian culture.

This book introduces you to a variety of the local drinks found in Peru. Most are national treasures and all are experiences worth having.

While we previously took a tour through regional drinks from Piura, Arequipa, and the Amazon, the following section highlights the iconic beverages of Lima: pisco sour (the national drink of Peru), the *chilcano* (a variation of the pisco sour), Inca Kola (the national soft drink), and Cusqueña Beer (a favorite local lager). Finally, we'll take a look at the unique fresh fruit juices of Peru.

The **Beverages** of Cusco section of this book puts a spotlight on six local beverages. While you can find these drinks in other cities, they have their roots from the Andes region. Some of these drinks were consumed from as early as the Inca Empire and others use herbs and plants from the Andes mountain range.

Collectively, all these unique Peruvian beverages add to the already rich gastronomical tapestry.

#1: Pisco Sour: The National Beverage of Peru

No exploration of the local Peruvian flavors would be complete without a taste of the country's national drink, pisco. The pisco sour is considered the national beverage of Peru and it even has its own National Holiday, celebrated on the first Saturday in February.

Pisco Sour is a cocktail that originated in Lima, Peru. It was invented in the early 1920s by an American bartender, Victor Vaughen Morris. In 1916, he opened Morris Bar in Lima and it quickly became a popular spot for Peruvian upper-class and English-speaking foreigners.

The pisco sour underwent several changes until Mario Bruiget, a Peruvian bartender working at Morris Bar, created the modern Peruvian recipe in the latter part of the 1920s by adding Angostura bitters and egg whites to the mix.

Pisco is a clear grape brandy that serves as the base liquor, and the cocktail includes lime juice, syrup, ice, egg white, and Angostura bitters.

The Pisco Sour War: Peruvian vs. Chilean Pisco Sour

Chile also claims the pisco sour as its national drink. There is much controversy between the two countries who each claim to be the birthplace of the Pisco Sour.

The Chilean version of the pisco sour is similar, but with a few notable differences. In Chile, the pisco sour is made with Chilean Pisco, sugar instead of syrup, and it excludes the bitters and egg whites.

Peruvian Pisco Sour

We tried our first pisco sour in Chile, and right away we got a sense of the rivalry between the two countries. Even in Peru, everywhere we enjoyed Peruvian pisco sour, there were always references made to the differences of the cocktail in the two countries.

Regardless of where it was invented or by whom, this cocktail remains a classic to be experienced.

A VISIT TO BODEGA RIVADENEYRA: THE OLDEST AUTHENTIC PERUVIAN PISCO BODEGA

Many of the Peruvian Pisco bodegas are found in the south of Peru, in the coastal valleys of Ica, Lima, Arequipa, Moquegua and Tacna. In 2012, the Ministry of Trade and Tourism instituted *la ruta del Pisco*, the official route of Pisco. The route starts in Lima and goes all the way to Tacna in the south of Peru.

We had the opportunity to visit **Rivadeneyra** [3], one of the oldest Pisco wineries, about three hours south of Lima, in a town called Lunahuana. This trip was organized by *Prensa Tur*, a magazine about Travel and Tourism in Peru.

Lunahuana is a popular destination not only for Pisco, but also for the landscape: it's a place to enjoy outdoor activities such as whitewater rafting, hiking and more.

The Tour

Bodega Rivadeneyra is a family-owned bodega that was created in 1756. Owner Julio Vidal Rivadeneyra guided our experience.

This bodega preserves its traditional and artisanal production processes. It also houses *Museo del Pisco*, a museum dedicated to pisco that exhibits bottles from bodegas across Lima, Arequipa, Tacna and Ica.

Pisco distillation alembic

As Pisco novices, we were fascinated by the fermentation and distillation processes. The fermentation *botijas* and distillation alembics were interesting to look at, although many of the nuances were lost to us, as the tour was given in Spanish.

The Four Main Types of Peruvian Pisco

- Pisco Puro is made exclusively from just one type of grape varietal, the most popular being the Quebranta grape varietal. At Rivadeneyra they make it using a non-aromatic grape, called Uvina (coming from the valley of Lunahuana). This is the perfect pisco for a pisco sour.

3 www.bodegarivadeneyra.pe

- Pisco Mosto Verde is made with a unique distillation process. This pisco is made with the green must of the grapes, which are taken to distillation before finishing the fermentation process. This results in a smoother, more velvety-tasting pisco. However, this requires twice the number of grapes that a Pisco Puro takes. Rivadeneyra makes the Pisco Verde Italia.
- Pisco Acholado is made with a blend of two or more types of grapes. Rivadeneyra makes a pisco combining 60% aromatic Italia grapes and 40% non-aromatic Uvina grapes.
- Pisco Aromatico is made from aromatic grapes, which tend to be floral and fruit-forward, providing an enhanced sensory experience. Italia and Moscatel are favorites for this type of pisco. Rivadeneyra makes the Pisco Italia, which has an aroma of flowers and fruit.

Pisco sours are delicious. They are subtly sweet, cool and refreshing for the heat of the long summer days. One thing to watch out for is how strong they are. The alcohol content in a pisco sour is between 38% and 48%. The fine balance between the intense citrus lime juice and sweetness of the sugar syrup makes it very easy to drink. Be careful and be warned; too many pisco sours can knock you off your feet!

#2: Chilcano

Like the pisco sour, the *chilcano* is a traditional Peruvian cocktail based on pisco, but it is not as strong. We were lucky enough to be in Lima during the *Semana del Chilcano,* an eleven-day festival in mid-January that celebrates this classic drink.

A *chilcano* is made with different fruit juices or soft drinks. A classic *chilcano* is made with pisco, preferably Quebranta, with lime juice, ginger ale, ice and Angostura bitters.

At the festival we discovered variations of the *chilcano* made with all kinds of exotic fruits like *maracuya* and *lúcuma* (see the Unique Local Fruits of Lima section). We enjoyed the *chilcano* and found it tasty and refreshing. While it may not be as popular as the pisco sour, it is a sweeter, less heavy alternative.

Add the *chilcano* to your drinking list in Peru and you'll be pleasantly surprised. You can try a Chilcano at anywhere you can find a Pisco Sour.

Spotlight
Where to Have Pisco Sour in Lima

There is no shortage of places to enjoy a pisco sour in Lima. Not being connoisseurs, we've compiled this list by asking a few *limeños* for their top favorite places to enjoy a pisco sour in Lima:

- **Antigua Taberna Queirolo** is also known locally as "El Queirolo". This always-busy bar is located a few blocks from the Museo Larco and the Museo Nacional de Historia en Pueblo Libre, making it a nice stop before or after museums visits.

    Address: *Av. San Martín 1090 Pueblo Libre, Lima Perú*

    Hours: *Every day, 8:00 am – 11:00 pm*

    Website: www.antiguatabernaqueirolo.com

- **Gran Hotel Bolivar** has a great view over the Plaza San Martín. Go there for the historical feel and the classic pisco sour called La Catedral: a double-sized pisco sour.

    Address: *Jirón de la Unión 958, Lima Lima 1*

    Hours: *Every day, 24 hours*

    Website: www.granhotelbolivar.com.pe

- **Pisco Bar** in Miraflores was recognized as the best bar for pisco by the Oenologic Club Magia del Pisco in 2015.

    Address: *Av. Petit Thouars # 5390 - Miraflores*

    Hours: *Tuesday to Thursday, 12:00 pm – 10:00 pm; Saturday and Sunday, 12:00 pm – 1:00 am*

    Website: www.piscobar.pe

- **Superba** is a quaint and charming bar in San Isidro, close to where we stayed in Lima. It has a bistro feel, amazing food and a nice selection of artisanal beers.

    Address: *Av. Petit Thouars, 2884, San Isidro*

    Hours: *Monday to Thursday, 12:00 pm – 11:00 pm; Friday and Saturday, 12:00 pm – 1:00 am*

    Website: www.superbarestaurant.com

#3: Inca Kola: Peru's Iconic Soft Drink

In countries like the U.S. it's either Coca-Cola or Pepsi; in Peru, it's only Inca Kola. Inca Kola is a strange-looking fluorescent yellow drink adorning tables in restaurants and homes all across Peru.

Super sweet with a bubblegum taste, Inca Kola is Peruvians' drink of choice to accompany meals.

Delicious chilcano

You'll find it in different types of eateries from fast food to *cevicherías*, *chifa* restaurants and more. Wherever you are in Peru, a glass of Inca Kola is never too far away.

The story of Inca Kola is fascinating and it speaks to the Peruvian sense of national identity. The origins of Inca Kola go back to 1910, when José Robinson Lindley and his wife Martha, a young English couple, opened a small shop in Lima to sell their homemade carbonated beverages. In 1935, Lima was celebrating 400 years since its founding, and the Lindleys decided to produce a unique drink to commemorate the event and their new homeland.

Marketed as the "Pride of Peru", the drink gained popularity in Lima and eventually gained a foothold to become the leader of the soft drinks industry in Peru. After years of unsuccessfully trying to dominate the Peruvian market, Coca-Cola eventually entered a strategic alliance with Inca Kola in 1999. Today, Inca Kola is part of the Coca Cola family and you can find it in many Peruvian restaurants and Latin-themed stores in the U.S.

#4: Cusqueña Beer

Although pisco sour is Peru's national drink, beer surpasses it in popularity. Peru has three major beer brands: Pilsen Callao, Cristal and Cusqueña. Pilsen Callao and Cristal are both lagers with little flavor in Claire's opinion (Rosemary is not a beer drinker).

Cusqueña makes several varieties of beers: golden lager, red lager, wheat beer, and dark lager. There is a beer for every taste, including the Cusqueña Quinua Beer. This beer is co-created with Gastón Acurio, Peru's top chef. It is a blend of pearl quinoa, malted barley, corn,

Inca Kola

hints of orange and peach, hops and natural pure water.

Claire enjoyed drinking Cusqueña Beer and could not wait to try the Quinua Special Edition. She found it slightly fruity and not too hoppy. The actual taste of quinoa was difficult to detect as it was hidden behind the barley and hop flavors. Nonetheless, it is easy to drink and worth trying on your travels to Peru.

Collection of Cusqueña beers

#5: Peruvian Fresh Juices and "Jugo Especial"

Peru is a paradise for unique fruits, and one of the best ways to enjoy the flavors is in fresh juices and smoothies. You will find fresh juice stands everywhere, and most restaurants offer fresh juices on their menus.

The choices of fruits are endless and include bananas, papayas, pineapples, guavas, *maracuya* (passionfruit) and many more. The juices are often sweetened with raw honey, *algarrobina* (carob extract) and fruit nectars. The fresh fruits, bright colors and fragrances are an intoxicating reminder of Mother Earth's goodness.

Jugo Especial
This hidden specialty is as thick as a meal in itself. It is a mix of a little bit of everything including Cusqueña beer (optional) and an egg.

We tried *jugo especial* at the local market for breakfast. Given it was early in the morning, we decided to skip the beer and egg extras. We enjoyed a deliciously thick juice big enough to share.

Unique Fruits and Produce

Peru has a variety of exotic fruits, many of which are superfoods rich in vitamins, and nutrients; many are said to cure diseases and ailments, including cancer.

The three distinct climates—*Costa* (the coast), *Selva* (the Amazon), and *Sierra* (the mountains)—produce many affordable and mouthwatering fresh fruits.

Highlighted below are some of the unique fruits we discovered. We have focused on the ones that were new to us and different from some we had eaten in Chile while discovering the local and authentic foods.

For instance, *paltas* or avocados are absolutely fantastic in Peru and you don't want to miss them. The creamy custardy taste of *chirimoya* or custard apples should not be missed. The same goes for *guayabas* or guavas, which are originally from Mexico and very popular in South America.

The following list includes ten fruits introduced to us by the locals, as well as others we stumbled upon. You will find most of these fruits throughout Peru, although some might be easier to find than others.

This list is by no means representative of all the fruits in Peru. We share this list as an interesting starting place to discover the incredible range of fruits and flavors available.

#1: Lúcuma

Known as "the last gold of the Incas," *lúcuma* is a subtropical fruit popular in Peru. We first discovered it in Chile and were immediately seduced by its delicious caramel flavors.

The *lúcuma* fruit is about the size of a small orange, with a succulent green-brownish skin. Inside, the flesh is golden in color and with a delicate, caramel-custard-like flavor that is hard to compare to other

Lúcuma

fruits. It has a unique texture that melts in the mouth with flavors similar to almond paste.

In addition to the delicious taste, *lúcuma* is rich in antioxidants, fiber, vitamins, beta-carotene and flavonoids.

This is one of the most delicious fruits we've ever eaten and we could not get enough while in Peru. Neither can Peruvians: *lúcuma* is Peru's favorite ice cream flavor, and it is used in yogurt, desserts, cakes and more. Whatever you do, don't miss lúcuma fruits on your travels to Peru!

#2: Pitahaya

Also known as dragon fruit, this was one of our favorites. The dragon fruit comes in several colors. Pink dragon fruit has pink or white flesh, and it's the most popular color, but we preferred the yellow with white flesh for its consistently sweet flavors. The fruit on the inside resembles a kiwi and the black seeds are edible. The fruit is sweet and very refreshing. It is known to be rich in vitamins C, B1, B2 and B3 as well as iron, calcium and phosphorus.

Pitahaya

#3: Pacay

This unusual fruit resembles a humongous green bean. Pacay is also called "ice cream bean" due to its sweet flavor and smooth texture. The inside looks like cotton, and although the pods are long, there is not much to eat inside once the seeds are taken out. What you eat is the white flesh, which is quite sweet and chewy. This fruit provides dietary fiber, which helps with getting rid of cholesterol and fat.

Pacay

#4: Cocona

In the section about **Amazon Cuisine**, we talked about Cocona juice. The juice comes from a colorful fruit, about the size of a small red pepper, that can be yellow, orange or red.

The fruit is actually quite bitter, so this fruit is usually consumed as a juice. The flesh on the

Cocona

inside is yellow with white edible seeds, and it is rich in iron and Vitamin B5. Enjoy the flavors in a juice alongside your meal.

#5: Camu Camu

This is another fruit that was previously mentioned in the **Amazon Cuisine** section. Like *cocona,* it is best consumed as a juice and not as a fruit.

These small fruits are the size of grapes, and very bitter. *Camu camu* has the highest Vitamin C intake of any fruit. The juice is citrusy, very easy to drink, and a great way to boost your immune system.

Camu Camu

#6: Maracuya

Maracuya fruits are in the same family as passionfruit or *granadilla*. We enjoyed fresh passionfruit on our quest in Chile, and we were eager to try the Peruvian version.

What we didn't know is that *maracuya* are never eaten plain—they're incredibly sour. Before we discovered this, we bought a couple, intrigued by their firm yellow and black shell. Once we cut into the *maracuya* and the yellow flesh with black seeds emerged, we dug in eagerly.

They were lip-puckering. We were shocked and surprised at how tart they were. Though they have benefits on their own (they're high in fiber, iron, phosphorus and vitamins C and B), they are best enjoyed as a mixed juice with pineapple. They're also lovely in a *maracuya* pisco sour.

Maracuya

#7: Tumbo

Tumbo fruit is known as banana passionfruit because of its shape: *tumbo* is similar to a short banana with rounded ends. The bright yellow rind has orange flesh inside that is very tart.

Tumbo

While it's not very enjoyable on its own, on the positive side, *tumbo* is low in calories and rich in vitamins A, B and C, as well as minerals like calcium and phosphorus.

#8. Aguaje

In the **Amazon Cuisine** section, we were introduced to *aguajina* juice, where it was described as a "female-only drink" due to its content of phytohormones, which mimic oestrogen hormones.

We stumbled upon this strange-looking fruit at the market and were surprised by its texture. The fruit is about the size of a large egg, and the skin is scaly on the outside. Once you peel the skin you discover yellow flesh surrounding a large hard nut.

Aguaje

When we tried the yellow flesh, we found it bitter and not very tasty. It was clear why it's not eaten as a fruit and enjoyed as a juice instead. The fruit comes from the moriche palm trees, native to the jungle. It is rich in vitamins, antioxidants, phytoestrogens, electrolytes and more.

#9: Mamey Sapote

We discovered the *mamey sapote* fruit purely by chance while walking in downtown Lima on our way to explore Barrio Chino (Chinatown).

On our way, we noticed a stand of fruits that looked like melons, tended by a young boy. We'd never seen these large orange fruits before, and the boy, Juan, explained that they were called *mamey sapote*. We bought one to taste.

The flesh inside was yellow, with a large brown seed in the middle. The taste was mild, and somewhat similar to a pumpkin: sweet, with a firm texture.

Mamey sapote is an excellent source of vitamin B6 and vitamin C, as well as source of vitamin B, vitamin E, manganese, potassium and dietary fiber.

Mamey Sapote

#10: Noni

This was by far one of the strangest fruits from the Amazon we discovered. We first saw it at the Surquillo Farmers' Market in Lima. We looked at an ugly, unappetizing, pale green tuber, and the vendor approached us and told us it was a fruit.

She went on to proclaim it as a "cancer killer". Not only is it unappetizing to look at, it also has a pungent

Noni

smell. We learned that is eaten cooked, primarily in stews. Even though we didn't get a chance to taste it, if you have the opportunity on your travels to Peru, it is worth sampling it for all the health benefits.

Local Markets

#1: Mercado de Surquillo #1

Surquillo Farmers' Market #1, known in Spanish as *Mercado de Surquillo #1*, is the most important food market in Lima.

The market is housed in a huge circular building. Fruits and vegetables line the outer circle. The inner core is mostly made up of butcher stands.

Unusual fruits and vegetables unlike what you've ever seen or heard of will assault your senses from every direction. Cacao from the Amazon, more quinoa varieties than you can imagine, potatoes of every shape and color, and watermelons the size of your thumb are a few of the fascinating items that will captivate you.

The butcher counters on the interior are especially remarkable. They are unlike the sanitized markets you may be accustomed to. Prepare yourself for whole chickens hanging by their feet with their necks slit open, a range of organ meats hanging on hooks, and giant pig's trotters, all out in the open.

Within the market are a number of food stalls. The majority of them focus on fresh seafood and *ceviche* right from the Pacific ocean. Our favorite seafood for *ceviche* was *El Rinconcito de Alex*.

Every Sunday, on the periphery around the market is the *Bioferia*, where only organic products are sold. Popular with locals, this is a perfect stop for those looking to eat or cook vegetarian, vegan or gluten-free while in Lima.

Beautiful display of fresh fruits

#2: Mercado de Surquillo #2

A few blocks down from Mercado #1 is a low single-story building taking up a city block or two. This market is much more local and not as popular with tourists.

While Mercado #1 focuses mostly on food, Mercado #2 is much more mixed, with everything from produce and meats to household goods, clothing, toys, antique furniture and more.

The food selection at this market is much larger, with several food stands offering a variety of local dishes.

The pedestrian mall around Mercado de Surquillo has been dubbed the *Boulevard Gastronomico de Surquillo,* or "Boulevard of Cuisine", to showcase Peru's epicurean heritage. This market is a must-stop on your travels to Peru and a great introduction to the diversity of Peruvian gastronomy.

Location: *Mercado de Surquillo*

Address: *Surquillo 15047*

Hours: *Monday to Friday, 7:00 am – 7:00 pm; Saturday and Sunday, 7:00 am – 4:00 pm*

Tip: *Go for lunch.*

#3: Mercado Central

The *Mercado Central,* or Central Market, is about five blocks from *Plaza des Armas* downtown and close to Barrio Chino (Chinatown). This is one of the largest markets and it occupies a whole block and stretches along a wide area.

This local market is busy, and the alleys are packed all day. At this market you can buy just about anything. Fruit and food stalls surround the market on all sides. Inside the main building are the fresh foods, with rows and rows of butchers as well as household goods.

The biggest obstacle is navigating your way around this massive market. Plan to spend the better part of the day exploring the market and the surrounding area. With the amount of people crowded in this space, leave your valuables behind.

Location: Mercado Central
Address: Jirón Ucayali 615, Cercado de Lima
Hours: Every day, 7:00 am – 10:00 pm
Tip: Taste the anticuchos at sundown.

#4: Terminal Pesquero: Lima's Largest Fish Market

Located southeast of Lima, the Villa Maria Del Triunfo District is home to the largest bustling fish market. The day starts before dawn and closes after 8:00 a.m. You'll find chefs and cooks from all types of establishments next to families buying the freshest catch of the day at incredibly low prices.

The variety of fish and seafood on display is unimaginable, with hundreds of live crabs, giant fish, sharks, clams, and mussels. Essentially, anything that lives in the sea is available here on bed of ice.

One of the best experiences is to make your own fresh *ceviche*. You can buy your own *corvina* (sea bass), have it cleaned, and then take it upstairs to the canteen. There you can choose a *cevicheria* to fillet your fish and minutes later you'll be breakfasting on the freshest *ceviche* in town.

The floors here are wet and the fish smell will stick to your shoes; be sure to wear rubber boots or some type of high or tall shoes. Nonetheless, this is a fascinating experience and you'll have a newfound appreciation of the incredible freshness and detail that goes into making Lima's famous *ceviche*.

Location: Terminal Pesquero
Address: Av. Pachacutec at the corner with Av. Maria Parado de Bellido Villa Maria del Triunfo District, Lima
Hours: Every day, 5:30 am – 8:00 am
Tip: Wear rubber shoes and make your own ceviche!

CUSCO, PERU

Cusco: The Second Gastronomy City

A view of Cusco

Perched high in the mountains, Cusco has the best cuisine in the Peruvian Andes, and the second-best gastronomy, right behind Lima.

Cusco is the former capital of Inca Empire and a Unesco World Heritage Site. It is one of Peru's most visited cities for Machu Picchu, the Sacred Valley of the Incas and other Inca heritage sites.

Your trip to Cusco probably involves visiting these spectacular historic sites. While in Cusco, aim to go beyond the tourist-catered experiences, and eat among the locals, at local venues with local fare. We provide addresses to guide your culinary exploration.

While many of the flavors are unusual and unexpected, savoring the experience through the tastes and stories will give you a deeper appreciation for this unique regional cuisine.

Cusco Cuisine

Walking the cobblestone streets of Cusco, it is not unusual to see ladies in colorful Andean attire walking llamas and baby goats; this is a city with strong Andean culture.

Depending on season and time of day, you'll also see vendors out and about selling local snacks, herbs, grains, and drinks.

The cuisine is influenced by the intense geography of the Andes Mountains. The diet draws heavily on the native ingredients of potatoes, maize and meat. Soups and stews are among the most popular dishes, usually accompanied by a variety of local beverages.

The following section outlines the local dishes, drinks and desserts not to miss while in Cusco.

Authentic Specialties Not To Miss in Cusco

#1: Alpaca
#2: Chicharron
#3: Chiriuchu
#4: Cuy
#5: Rocoto Relleno
#6: Pachamanca

Local Beverages

#1: Chicha Morada
#2: Chicha Jora
#3: Chicha Frutilla
#4: Emoliente
#5: Maca
#6: Mate de Coca

Unique Produce & Ingredients from the Andes Region

#1: Aji Amarillo
#2: Choclo - Peruvian Corn
#3: Kiwicha
#4: Maiz Morado - Purple Corn
#5: Peruvian Potatoes
#6: Sal de Maras
#7: Quinoa

Local Markets

#1: San Pedro Market
#2: Chinchero Market
#3: Pisac Market
#4: Machu Picchu Market

Authentic Specialties Not to Miss in Cusco

#1: Alpaca

The alpaca is a domesticated species of South American camelid that looks like a small llama.

These two species, however, are raised for different purposes. The llama is used to transport products and goods, and the meat is tougher.

Alpacas are too small to be used as pack animals, and instead they're raised mostly for their meat and their fiber, which is used to make woven items, such as blankets, sweaters, gloves, and more.

Alpaca with rice and potatoes

The meat from the alpaca is tender—more so than the llama meat that we had experienced in the Northern part of Argentina. This is due to the fact that the alpaca is not used for transportation or carrying goods, therefore the meat is more tender.

The alpaca meat has the same properties as llama meat: high in protein and low in fat, making it a great alternative to beef for its low cholesterol intake.

We enjoyed the meat and found it mild in flavor, tender, and easy to slice: a nice change from beef.

Where to Try Alpaca

You can find *lomo de alpaca* (alpaca sirloin) in many restaurants in Cusco. We actually tried Alpaca on our way to Machu Picchu in the town of Aguas Calientes.

> **Location: Indio Feliz Restaurant** *(www.indiofeliz.com/franco-peruvian-cuisine-machupicchu-1-0)*
>
> **Address**: *Calle Lloque Yupanqui Nº 103, Aguas Calientes*
>
> **Hours:** *Every day, 12:00 pm – 10:00 pm*

#2: Chicharrón

Chicharrón is a local favorite popular throughout South America. This dish is originated in Spain and is part of the traditional cuisine of many countries with Spanish influence.

At its core, *chicharrón* is deep-fried pork from different cuts, including pork belly or pork rinds.

In Cusco, *chicharrón* is served with a blend of local ingredients on your plate: traditional Andean white corn, potatoes, onion, mint and lemon.

Unfortunately, we did not get a chance to try out this local speciality in Cusco. At the time, we were both suffering from a slight touch of the stomach flu and did not want to make to aggravate the situation further.

Nevertheless, when you find yourself in Cusco, do seek out the apparently delicious local specialty, *chicharrón*.

Chicharrón

Where to Try Chicharrón
In Cusco, we spotted the dish at a number of places around *Plaza des Armas,* the main square.

#3: Chiriuchu
Specialty of Cusco
As we asked around for other local food specialties to try in Cusco, our local hosts told us about *chiriuchu.*

Chiriuchu is a cold meal which literally means "spicy cold" in the Quechua language. It is a festive dish that is usually prepared in the month of June, during the celebration of Corpus Christi.

Though the Corpus Christi religious festival is celebrated throughout Peru, the largest and most spectacular celebrations are held in Cusco.

Central to the celebration are the fifteen adorned statues representing saints and religious figures. Sixty days after Easter Sunday, these life-size statues are taken to Cusco Cathedral from their respective parishes (some of them seven miles away) in order to "greet" the body of Christ. Specially-chosen bearers carry the saints upon their shoulders in processions which often last an entire day.

In the evening, everyone enjoys the traditional meal of *chiriuchu* which combines elements from different nearby regions.

The true origins of *chiriuchu* date back even further to the Inca Empire. Villagers from various regions of the Inca Empire would come to Cusco with their food specialties and participate in religious processions.

The name for this celebration is *Inti Raymi*, the Inca Festival of the Sun. It was a tribute to the venerated Sun God Inti and was created by Emperor Pachacutec.

When the Spanish conquistadors arrived in Cusco in the 16th century, they enforced the festival of Corpus Christi on the natives in a bid to overshadow the traditional Inca festival of Inti Raymi. Today, both Corpus Christi and Inti Raymi are celebrated in Cusco within just a few weeks of each other.

Chiriuchu combines several specialties from the coast, the highlands and the Amazon. The specialties are: *cuy* (guinea pig), *chorizo* (sausage), *gallina* (hen), *cecina or charki* (dried meat), *cochayuyo* (seaweed), *maiz* (corn), *torreja* (a type of omelette with corn flour, potatoes, yellow squash, green onions, and spices), *huevas de pescado* (fish eggs), *queso* (cheese) and *cancha* (toasted, crunchy corn).

All the ingredients are piled on top of each other, with hot peppers at the very top. We had *chiriuchu* at a *picantería* where locals converge to have this traditional meal. This experience by itself opened us up to the Peruvian Andean culture, the local habits and the surprising flavors of the food.

Chiriuchu

Where to Try Chiriuchu

Unless you are in Cusco in June where *chiriuchu* is served in many eateries, you will need to find a specialty restaurant to try this dish.

We went to La Cusquenita, a *tradicional picantería* (traditional restaurant serving meat) in Cusco to experience it. The place was recommended to us by our local host, Doris. It is a large dining room where locals converge to have a traditional meal. Here, you can find several traditional dishes from the Cusco region such as the *cuy* (guinea pig), *caldo de gallina* (chicken soup), *chicharrón* (fried pork) *and trucha frita* (fried trout).

The *chiriuchu* was a bit spicy, but made tolerable by the corn and cheese. The dish was served cold, which took away from the flavors of the different cuts of meats and poultry. The most interesting part of the meal was having fish eggs and seaweed as well. This unique dish with unusual combinations is full of history and an experience not to be missed in Cusco.

Location: La Cusquenita *(www.facebook.com/lacusquenitapicanteria)*

Address: *Av. Centenario 800 and Av. De La Cultura (Puente Marcavalle), Cusco*

Hours: *Monday to Saturday, 11:00 am – 10:30pm; Sunday, 11:00 am – 6:00 pm*

#4: Cuy - Guinea Pig

Available everywhere in Cusco

There is no other single Peruvian dish that generates such a visceral reaction. Guinea pig or *cuy* (pronounced COOee) is a delicacy that must to be mentioned.

Cuy are essentially guinea pigs. A species of rodents belonging to the *Cavia Porcellus* family. In Western societies, guinea pigs are popular household pets. In South America and in the Andes region, *cuy* are an important food source among indigenous groups. Ancient Peruvians supplemented their diet with guinea pig and this custom still exists today.

We were not particularly excited about trying this furry animal, we knew we needed to as part of our quest for authentic and local specialties.

Where To Try Cuy

Dotted along Plaza des Armas (the main square in Cusco) are a number of restaurants catering to tourists, with large flashy menus and signs proclaiming to have the best in *cuy* in town.

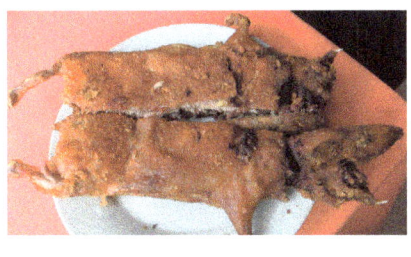
Cuy - Guinea Pig

When exploring the local foods, we avoid these types of restaurants; they scream "tourist trap", offering shocking experiences with no respect for the food, but rather an attraction for tourist dollars.

At the guidance of our local Airbnb hosts, we went to an off-the-beaten path restaurant located in a residential area. This restaurant, Cuyeria Sabor Moqueguano, only makes one dish: *cuy*.

There are two main ways in which *cuy* is prepared: *cuy al horno* (baked *cuy*) or *cuy chactado* (fried *cuy*). Our hosts recommended that we try *cuy chactado,* which is the cooking technique used in Arequipa (Peru's second most populous city), where *cuy* is said to have started.

The *cuy* was served with potatoes and *rocoto relleno* (fried stuffed peppers) which are also unique to Arequipa.

How to Eat Cuy

Not knowing if we would like the taste, we ordered one *cuy* to share between us. When we got our *cuy* our first question was *how do we eat it?* We looked around the restaurant to see how the locals were doing it. This is not a knife-and-fork meal. This is the kind of dish where you get your hands dirty. The bones are really thin and brittle, and your hands are the best bet.

The Taste of Cuy

Everyone says that strange new meats "taste like chicken", but this is not the case with *cuy*. It is a dark meat, very lean, with surprisingly little meat on the bones.

After biting into it several times, the closest thing we could come up with is that it tastes like rabbit, though, not exactly; it's not too gamey.

Honestly, we didn't find it to have much meat, or any distinctive flavor, but it was a distinctly weird experience biting into a whole guinea pig, with its mouth, teeth, legs and all. All in all, it is a once-in-a-lifetime experience. (We emphasize *once*!)

Location: **Cuyeria Sabor Moqueguano**

Address: 28 de Julio, Tercer Paradero, Cusco

Hours: Tuesday to Sunday, 11:30am – 5:00 pm

#5: Rocoto Relleno
Available everywhere in Cusco

Rocoto relleno is a hot, delicious and unique Peruvian dish. The *rocoto* is a chili of Andean origin that has been used for over 5,000 years. It looks very similar to a red bell pepper, but it doesn't taste like one: it is fiery hot—some say it is about 50 times spicier than a jalapeño.

Similar to a stuffed pepper, *rocoto relleno* is made from a large oval shaped *rocoto* pepper stuffed with a mixture of chopped beef and pork, mixed with diced onions, sliced hard-boiled eggs, and seasoned with *ají panca* chili paste, cumin, salt and pepper. The peppers are topped with cheese and baked.

Rocoto Relleno

This traditional dish is often enjoyed as an appetizer. However, in Arequipa, *rocotos rellenos* and scalloped potatoes are eaten together as a traditional pairing.

Locals say *rocotos rellenos* represent the fiery Misti volcano from the Arequipa region.

Get ready for a deeply satisfying dish full of burning traditions.

#6: Pachamanca
Available everywhere in Cusco

Pachamanca is a traditional way of cooking that has been used in the Andes for centuries, and it is still very popular all over the Andean region.

The name *pachamanca* is the combination of two words in the local Quechua language: "*pacha*" for earth, and "*manca*" for cooking pot. *Pachamanca* could be translated as "earth oven".

For the Incas, *pachamanca* was tied to ritual. More than a method of cooking, a *pachamanca* was a celebration in and of itself; a source of fertility and life.

Seasoned meat, herbs and vegetables are placed underground on a bed of hot stones, to be slowly cooked for many hours.

Ingredients are organized according to their cooking times. A mixture of native potatoes and sweet potatoes make the base layer. The second layer is reserved for marinated meats, such as beef, pork, lamb, guinea pig or chicken. Intertwined are more heated stones and a layer of herbs. The top and final layer is for corn, Andean cheese, *humitas* and cooked beans.

The hole in the ground is covered with leaves and dirt and allowed to cook anywhere from two to four hours.

Cooking food underground pays homage to Pachamama, an Incan goddess also referred to as Mother Earth. Food is returned to the earth's belly before eating, as a sign of respect.

Today, *pachamanca* is still widely eaten in Peru. Even though the ingredients vary by region, it is still the centerpiece of many Peruvian gatherings in the Andes.

More than a meal, a *pachamanca* is a ritual that gives a unique opportunity to get a glimpse of life led by the Incas.

Beverages

Like the food, the drinks in Cusco draw on the rich variety of natural resources. Many of these drinks are difficult to find outside of Peru, and they are also best enjoyed in their local environment.

The high altitude of the Andes will have you reaching for *mate de coca* to help with altitude sickness. A serving of thick *emoliente* will help you with other ailments. Perhaps you simply want to try one of the ancient Incan concoctions, like *chicha morada*. As you become familiar with new tastes, branch out and and try each of these local beverages.

#1: Chicha Morada

Chicha morada is a traditional and typical drink made from purple corn, a unique variety native to Peru. The drink has a long history, and has been said to date back prior to the creation of the Inca Empire.

This non-alcoholic beverage is made by boiling the purple corn with pineapple skin, cinnamon, cloves, and sugar. Purple corn is high in anthocyanins, which have many health benefits including reduced risk of heart disease and lower blood pressure.

This was one of our favorite beverages to go along with our meals. We

Chicha Morada

found it deliciously sweet and refreshing; the cinnamon adds a bright spark to the tongue. With its intriguing deep purple color, we could not resist all the goodness contained in this unique Peruvian drink.

#2: Chicha de Jora

Chicha de jora is a traditional drink from the Andes and it that comes from the Inca Empire period. It is similar to a beer, and made out of *jora*, a type of yellow corn from the Andes.

Traditionally, to make *chicha*, the first step is to chew up the corn and spit it into the brewing vessel. Like malting, this converts the starch into fermentable sugars. In Peru, *chicha* is traditionally made by women.

Chicha de Jora

We discovered *chicha de jora* while having lunch at the market in Chinchero, a small Andean village in the Sacred Valley. In a huge pot, surrounded by elderly ladies dressed in traditional Andean bright colors, was a bubbling liquid with a fermentation foam on the top. We had heard it was made by spitting into the drink, but did not notice the ladies spitting at that time.

Chicha de jora was the only beverage available to accompany our lunch. It was served in a large plastic glass, impossible to hold with one hand. We later learned the glass has a special name: *kero*.

The drink has a layer of thick foam on the top of the glass. We learned that it is tradition to spill the first portion of the beverage on the ground, saying, "*Pachamama, santa tierra*," as an offering to Mother Earth (*Pachamama* in Quechua).

The first taste was slightly sweet, but the drink finished with a strong sour taste, similar to a bitter apple cider. We barely finished it!

Traditionally, *chicha de jora* was a favorite drink of the Inca. You won't find it served at restaurants, though it is extremely popular with the locals. In the Peruvian highlands, it is also used as a ceremonial beverage during festivities to honor Inca gods.

#3: Chicha de Frutilla

Chicha de frutilla, also known as *frutillada,* is a sweeter version of *chicha de jora*. It is made with *frutilla* (strawberries) and sugar, which are both blended into *chicha de jora*.

This pink iced drink tastes much sweeter than the *chicha de jora*. The strawberries cover the bitter taste, which makes it much more drinkable than the *chicha de jora*.

We had our first *frutillada* at a traditional *picantería* (traditional restaurant) in Cusco. Like at the market, the beverage was served in an enormous glass that was only possible to hold with two hands. It still took some effort to finish the glass, but we much preferred this sweetened version.

#4: Emoliente

Emoliente is one of the most unique Peruvian drinks we discovered by chance. Rosemary was not feeling very well in Cusco, and our Airbnb host told us about a natural healing drink called *emoliente* sold at street corners by vendors called *emolienteras*. We had seen these carts appear every evening and had been very curious about them.

We approached a friendly-looking vendor one evening, eager to try this natural cure. *Emoliente* is like an herbal tea, popular during the cold season. It is prepared with a base of herbs that usually includes barley, dried horsetail, flax seed, plantain leaf and alfalfa sprouts.

On the vendor's cart were two big covered bowls and several intriguing pharmaceutical-like bottles on the side.

The vendor told us that the five or six bottles on the side were liquids with healing properties, made from natural plants from the Andes Mountains.

Emoliente vendor

The vendor put the main *emoliente* in a glass for Rosemary, and added in about 3 shots of natural liquids to help with stomach flu and indigestion. The first sip was a little bizarre: the drink was fruity, yet slimy, like there was a coating on the liquid. It was not disgusting, but it was unlike anything we have ever tasted before; imagine drinking a hot, fruity, slimy and semi-sparkling beverage.

Nonetheless, the drink went down quite easily and Rosemary felt much better taking something natural over prescription drugs. In addition to drinking *emoliente* hot, it can also be consumed as a cold drink.

Though traditionally sold on street corners, you can find *emoliente* in bars, restaurants and even *emoliente* tea bags in grocery stores in Peru.

Where to Try
Look for the *emolienteras* on busy street corners starting at 5pm in major cities, or try the following trendy *emoliente* bar in Miraflores, Lima.

La Emolientería

Address: Diagonal 598, Miraflores 15074, Lima

#5: Maca

One morning in Cusco, while having breakfast with Doris, our local host, she mentioned *maca* as a beverage that most Peruvians drink in the morning. Our interest immediately perked up as she pulled a brownish-yellow powder out of her kitchen cupboard.

Maca is a root vegetable that grows in central Peru in the high plateaus of the Andes Mountains. This radish relative has been cultivated for over 2,600 years. Growing at about 10,000 feet above sea level, it is the highest altitude crop in the world.

Peruvian *maca* is said to have played a central part in the Incan diet. As the Incas were building Machu Picchu, they relied on *maca* for energy to move the heavy blocks to construct Machu Picchu. The legendary strength of the Inca warriors has also been attributed to eating copious amounts of *maca* before going into battle.

Maca in powder format

At the markets, we quickly discovered three types of *maca*: black *maca* for men, yellow *maca* for women, and red *maca*, which is more expensive and difficult to find.

As we tried to understand what makes *maca* special, we ran up against some conflicting information between what the local Peruvians told us and what we found online.

Local Peruvian women told us they experienced many benefits with *maca*. They explained that *maca* gave them more energy and clearer skin. It is used to stop hair loss, help with hormonal imbalance (menstrual irregularities and menopause), arouse sexual desire, and boost the immune system. The Peruvians we spoke to told us that *maca* fights osteoporosis, depression, stomach cancer, leukemia, HIV/AIDS, and tuberculosis.

An internet search on WebMD revealed that *maca* is used for "tired blood" (anemia), chronic fatigue syndrome, and enhanced energy, stamina, athletic performance, memory, and fertility.

We first tried *maca* at the Mercado San Pedro in Cusco. The vendor told us that locals like to add *maca* powder to their tea or coffee, but she personally preferred it plain with hot water.

We took her recommendation to try it pure, and we enjoyed the chalky texture and interesting taste.

How Maca Works

According to Wikipedia, the *maca* root is an adaptogen. This means that it promotes homeostasis and stabilization of the body. For example, if one person is high in a specific hormone (such as oestrogen), *maca* will assist that person's body to lower the amount of oestrogen in their blood. However, if another person is low in the same hormone, it will assist that person's body to increase the amount of it in their blood.

Maca is said to stimulate the hypothalamus and pituitary glands, which regulate the other glands in the body, and can bring balance to the adrenal, thyroid, pancreas, ovarian and testicular glands.

After hearing so much about the benefits of *maca*, Rosemary decided to put herself on a 30-day Peruvian *maca* diet.

ROSEMARY'S 30-DAY PERUVIAN MACA DIET

The diet was simple: drink one cup of *maca* every day and see how the body responds. Rosemary bought one kilo of yellow *maca* at the Surquillo Farmers' Market in Lima. The plan was to drink *maca* every day between 3pm – 6pm.

While Peruvians drink *maca* in the morning, Rosemary would not give up her morning cup of coffee. Given that *maca* is said to be energizing, Rosemary thought drinking *maca* in the late afternoon when she sometimes needed a pick-me-up would be a great way to test the benefits. Nothing else changed in her diet, and she continued to exercise on a regular basis.

The Changes Experienced

- **Increased energy:** Just after two or three days of drinking *maca*, Rosemary felt much more energetic. The afternoon fatigue practically disappeared. The boost in energy was more than just physical; she felt mentally alert and focused as well. She noticed this after about five to seven days.

- **Less menstrual pain:** Even though Rosemary doesn't have a horrible period in terms of pain or any issues, she felt much more even, with no mood swings, no cramping and no anxiety. While on her period, she felt and performed as if she was not on her menstrual cycle.

- **Clearer skin:** About fifteen days or so into the experiment, Rosemary was surprised when looking at the mirror while washing her face. Her skin felt smoother and clearer, with no breakouts or spots. What a pleasant surprise, given that she never changed her facial or grooming habits.

- **Stronger hair and nails:** Before the *maca* diet, Rosemary would cut her nails every four to six weeks. While taking *maca*, that frequency increased and her nails were harder and stronger. Just like the nails, her hair felt stronger, with less breakage.

Any Downsides?

- **No negative impact noted.** Rosemary did not observe any negative effects from being on the 30-day Maca diet. Instead, she happily incorporated the natural supplement into her diet after the end of the 30-day period.

Note: Before embarking on a maca diet, please consult your doctor or medical professional.

#6: Mate de Coca: The Altitude Sickness Cure

Famous in the Andes region, *mate de coca* is a very popular treatment for altitude sickness. It is an herbal tea made from the leaves of the coca plant.

We first had *mate de coca* in Cusco to help us adapt to the high altitude, 11,200 feet (3,400 meters) above sea level.

However, this tea is controversial.

According to Wikipedia, the leaves from the coca plant contain alkaloids, which when extracted chemically are the source for cocaine. Though the amount in the coca alkaloids in the leaves is small, one cup of coca tea can cause a positive result on a drug test for cocaine.

Though illegal in the U.S., coca tea is legal in Colombia, Peru, Bolivia, Argentina, Ecuador and Chile.

Mate de Coca

Controversy aside, we enjoyed this unique Peruvian drink. We found it easy to drink, with a green-tea taste. *Mate de coca* not only kept us acclimatized, but it also kept us warm in the cold weather.

If your travels take you to Cusco, Peru, stop by the Coca Museum for more about coca leaves, which were sacred to the Incas, and used as a natural remedy for many ailments.

Location: *Museo de La Coca*

Address: *Plazoleta San Blas 618 Cusco Peru*

Hours: *Every day, 8:00 am – 8:00 pm*

Unique Local Fruits and Produce

Much of the unique produce in Peruvian cuisine comes from the rich Andes region. Many of these ingredients, like quinoa, have gained popularity worldwide for their nutritional benefits.

This section is not an attempt to cover them all, but instead put a spotlight on the popular and unique produce you will encounter on your travels to Peru.

#1: Ají Amarillo

The most frequently used chili in Peru, *ají amarillo* is probably the most important ingredient in Peruvian cooking. The chilis are native to the Andes, and ancient Peruvians relied on *ají*, in addition to salt and herbs, for seasoning their food.

Ají means chili pepper, and *amarillo* means yellow in Spanish. These medium-to-hot chilis start off green, but change to a bright orange as they mature.

Ají amarillo is used in many classic Peruvian dishes, such as *ají de gallina*, *papa a la huancaína* and more. It is also used in many sauces, where it adds a bright complex flavor as well as its distinctive yellowish-orange color.

Gastón Acurio branded Aji Amarillo Chili paste

The famous Peruvian chef Gastón Acurio even has his own line of Gastón Acurio branded *ají amarillo* chili paste.

#2: Choclo

Choclo, also known as Peruvian or Cusco corn, is an Andean corn with extra large, bulbous kernels. It is the main staple of Peru and has been part of the daily diet for thousands of years.

Of all the varieties of corn, *choclo* is the most popular and most consumed. The seeds are almost five times bigger than the sweet corn often consumed in the U.S. or Europe, and are white to creamy in color.

In Peru, *choclo* is eaten in a number of ways. You'll find it in soups (thick and light) and *tamales*, but the most popular way to eat *choclo* is simply boiled and served with a big hunk of *queso fresco* (a white cheese) or *queso serrano* (an Andean cheese).

CANCHA: ANDEAN POPCORN

At most restaurants in Peru, you'll get a bowl of *cancha* as a complimentary snack that will keep your fingers busy while waiting for your meal.

The corn is a special variety that doesn't pop like popcorn, but instead swells up into a sort of homemade corn nut. The kernels are toasted in a clay pot, and as soon as they start to crack open, salt is added.

Sometimes, *cancha* is added as a topping to *ceviche*, adding a nice crunchy contrast to the dish.

Beware; these can be highly addictive!

Addictive cancha

#3: Kiwicha

We were always struck by a strange grain that we would see in the markets next to the quinoa section. *Kiwicha* (pronounced kee-wee-cha), or amaranth, is an ancient crop cultivated for thousands of years by the Incas of the Andes.

The poppy-sized grains of *kiwicha* are noted for their dense nutritional content. *Kiwicha* is high in fiber and protein, and contains many vitamins and essential minerals. It is considered a superfood due to its antioxidant, anticarcinogenic, antihypertensive and antilipidemic properties. It is also touted to protect cardiac function, due to its ability to lower LDL, total cholesterol and triglycerides.

Kiwicha is a complete protein source and a wonderful alternative for vegetarians and vegans.

Kiwicha with other grains

This grain can be cooked like oatmeal or eaten as pilaf, and we enjoyed a delicious snack of energy bars made from popped *kiwicha*. When in Peru, add *kiwicha* to your diet to boost your health and vitality.

#4: Maiz Morado

Maiz morado (Spanish for purple corn) is one of the unique corn varieties native to Peru. It has a long history dating back prior to the creation of the Inca Empire.

At the local markets in Peru, you'll be struck by the unique color of this familiar crop. Purple corn is high in anthocyanins, which are miracle molecules found in dark-colored fruits and vegetables. They're being studied for their ability to improve everything from cardiovascular health to collagen regeneration. There have also been some very promising studies on their effects on cancer cells.

Maiz morado at the market

Purple corn is used to make the very popular drink *chicha morada* (see the **Beverages** of Cusco section for more), and the traditional dessert *mazamorra morada* (see the **Desserts** section for more).

#5: Peruvian Potatoes

South America is the birthplace of potatoes, and their origins can be traced to the Andes Highlands, on the border between present day Bolivia and Peru. The potato was domesticated over 10,000 years ago and quickly became an essential part of the Inca diet.

The potato is a crucial part of the culinary culture in Peru, with close to 4,000 unique varieties available in different sizes, shapes, colors, and textures. Because they all taste different, they are used in distinct recipes.

So important is this tuber that it even has its own holiday: National Potato Day is celebrated every May 30th all over Peru, with restaurants offering special menus using a variety of native Peruvian potatoes.

Peru is Latin America's top potato producer, as well as its promoter of native potatoes and potato products internationally. Potatoes today are the third most important food crop in the world, behind rice and wheat.

DISCOVERING NATIVE PERUVIAN POTATOES AT SAN PEDRO MARKET, CUSCO

San Pedro Market in Cusco is one of the most fascinating places to see the breadth and variety of Peruvian potatoes.

With black, yellow, red, white and purple potatoes, the color spectrum is amazing. While we had already seen *papas andinas* (native potatoes) in the north of Argentina, the unique variety of Peruvian potatoes we discovered in Cusco gave us an even deeper appreciation for the range of options available.

Discover and sample rescued varieties of potatoes and meet the producers who work hard to keep these varieties alive.

Peruvian Potatoes

Squiggly potatoes

EATING CHUÑOS - FREEZE-DRIED POTATOES

Trying some of the local and diverse varieties is part of the joy of traveling through local food.

At Chinchero Market, located about 30 kilometers from Cusco, we had the chance to try dehydrated potatoes.

Our visit was primarily to see a local Andean market as well as explore the nearby Inca ruins. We arrived in time for lunch and took the opportunity to sample the local specialties.

On the menu that day was deep-fried trout, served with two different kinds of potatoes and a small salad with slices of tomatoes on a bed of greens.

Local fish with freeze dried potatoes at Chinchero market

The two different kinds of potatoes were regular yellow potatoes and *chuños*: small, white, skinless freeze-dried potatoes. We much preferred the familiar taste of the regular yellow potatoes. We did not find the freeze-dried potatoes to be tasty at all. The texture was weirdly chewy, and they lacked flavor.

While we were not fans of the freeze-dried potatoes, learning about their history gave us a new appreciation for them. *Chuño* potatoes date back to the pre-Inca period. After harvest, small potatoes are selected and left overnight in low temperatures. During the day, they are exposed to bright sunlight, and crushed to extract more liquid and remove the skins. This process is repeated for three to five days. Before electricity and refrigeration, *chuño* potatoes could be stored for long periods of time.

You will not typically find *chuño* potatoes at fancy restaurants; the best place to see and try them is at the local markets.

#6: Sal de Maras

The pink salt of Maras in Peru has become a favored ingredient of Peruvian chefs, and a highlight of Peru's gastronomic boom.

The salt comes from the Sacred Valley between Cusco and Machu Picchu. Maras is home to an incredible network of ancient salt terraces that have been in use since before the Incas.

Warm salty water from a natural spring on the side of the mountain is cleverly directed into hundreds of shallow terraced ponds via an intricate system of narrow channels. The water is left to evaporate from these pools, leaving natural and unrefined salt in its place.

A cooperation-based system of work has been used by this community to harvest these salt ponds since their inception, and amazingly, this communal system is still in use.

The mineral-rich salt doesn't just add flavor to dishes; it's also good for you. It contains magnesium, iron, calcium and zinc, which help reduce stress and prevent anemia and osteoporosis. It provides a buffer for blood sugar levels, preventing diabetes and enabling diabetics to use less insulin.

Renowned Peruvian Chef Gastón Acurio put Maras on the map a few years ago when he raved about the salt and began using it in his dishes.

Rafael Piqueras, another Peruvian chef, loves the salt so much that he named his Lima restaurant "Maras".

Salt grinders filled with the pink salt can now be found on the dining tables of some of the country's top restaurants.

#7: Quinoa

Quinoa, or *quinua* in Spanish, is an amazing ancient superfood that is now being rediscovered worldwide. This "Golden Grain of The Andes" was a daily staple of the Incan diet more than 5,000 years ago. Since pre-Hispanic times, it has been cultivated across the entire Andean Mountain Range, including in Argentina, Bolivia, Chile, Colombia, Ecuador and Peru. Due to this sustained history, the United Nations dubbed 2013 the "International Year of Quinoa."

This grain was first grown in Bolivia, but today Peru is the largest producer. These two countries produce about 95% of all commercially grown quinoa. Loaded with protein, fiber, and minerals, this highly versatile and nutritious plant plays an important role in eradicating hunger and malnutrition.

In Peru, we were astonished at the how often the grains made their way into local dishes, desserts and drinks.

We were surprised by **quinoa bread**, which we found to be denser than regular wheat bread. **Quinoa milk** had the texture of soy milk.

Quinoa pasta was already familiar, and lighter on the stomach. We felt healthier eating the traditional *picarones* dessert (see **Desserts** section) which uses quinoa flour. And the most unexpected use of quinoa that we discovered was **Quinoa Beer.** (see the **Beverages** of Lima section for more).

Quinoa bread and grains

Local Markets

Andean villages surround Cusco, the historical capital of the former Inca Empire, and they stretch into the Sacred Valley where many important Inca ruins remain.

You will find many important open air markets with traditional Andean crafts, as well as local food speciality stands. These markets are easily accessible from Cusco.

This section highlights some of the main markets worth visiting, with a brief description as well as a few stories from our personal experience.

#1: Mercado San Pedro, Cusco

A short walk from Plaza de Armas, the main square in Cusco, you'll begin to see the bustling Mercado San Pedro. The crowds, noise, chaos, scents, and colors erupt in this huge market, which is unlike any clean and sanitized market found in North America or Europe. There is no better place to find the full diversity of local produce under one roof (and spilling into the sidewalks).

This traditional market is divided into several sections, which all have their own specialties. You will find the same offerings you typically expect from a farmers' market, with sections for cheese, meat, fruit, vegetables and flowers. However, at this market you will also find additional sections dedicated to the local specialties: a rainbow of native potatoes, varieties of Peruvian corn, quinoa, *maca* and *kiwicha* (see the **Unique Produce** of Cusco section for more). There is also a gastronomy section serving local and authentic dishes.

Set any expectations aside and immerse yourself in the local Andean culture at this market.

EATING AT SAN PEDRO MARKET

When you are on the quest for authentic food, as we are, you learn to work up the courage to eat in places that have a lower standard of hygiene than you are used to. With Cusco being a gastronomy city, and the market crowded with hundreds of locals eating lunch, we knew we could not go wrong. What we needed was our personal reminder: sometimes the tastiest food is usually served in not-so-inviting venues.

Lunch at San Pedro Market

Just like the rest of the market, the gastronomy section is also divided into sub-sections. Across from the potatoes aisle is a breakfast section with exotic fresh-squeezed juices like passion fruit, papaya, pineapple, cantaloupe and more.

The gastronomy section focuses on the local and traditional dishes. To taste some of Peru's most popular dishes, this is the place to go. The clang of pots and pans, the crackle of food cooking on hot stoves, and the clatter of plates being served and eagerly cleaned tempts the waiting crowds.

There is a system to the way lunch service works. Fortunately, our Airbnb hosts had prepared us in advance. The idea is to walk around the local speciality food stands. Find a menu that tempts you. Grab an open space on any of the long benches, sit down and wait to be served.

The lunch menu is fixed at 5 Peruvian Nuevo Sol (approx. $1.50 USD) and it includes a starter, main meal and fruit juice.

It was at this market where we enjoyed for the first time Peruvian specialties like *lomo saltado,* and the local Cusqueña soups, *caldo* or *sopa de gallina* (hen soup), or *sopa de pollo* (chicken soup). Despite the appearance of the place, the food was delicious and cooked right in front of our eyes. Go there for lunch with an empty belly and an open mind. There is no better way to taste the local food, alongside a slice of local life.

Location: *San Pedro Market, Cusco*

Hours: *Every day, 9:00 am – 6:00 pm*

Tip: *Go for lunch.*

#2: Chinchero Market, Sacred Valley

Chinchero is located about 30 kilometers away from Cusco. To get there, we took the local *collectivo* (bus) for a 45 minute trip. We were looking forward to seeing a market right outside of Cusco and experiencing the local food specialties.

You will find traditional handicrafts in vibrant colors and uniquely Peruvian designs. This area is famous for weaving and you may be able to see talented weavers demonstrating the process as well as the use of natural dyes.

Compared to San Pedro Market in Cusco, this market has very few food stands, but nonetheless serves the local fare. It was at this market where we tried *chicha jora* (see the **Beverages** of Cusco section), the traditional local beer.

Vendor at Chinchero Market

The Inca ruins in Chinchero are believed to have been the court residence of Inca leader Túpac Yupanqui. Looking out at the huge terraces, you can imagine the Incas cultivating different herbs and vegetables.

Chinchero is also traditionally believed to be the "Birthplace of the Rainbow." This has been attributed to its elevation, the traditional independence of the people of Chinchero, and the unique quality of the textiles they produce.

This market offers an unmatched experience that is worth the trip.

Location: *Chinchero Market, in the Sacred Valley between Cusco and Urubamba*

Address: *Ruta Santisimo Downhill 2, Urubamba, Peru*

Hours: *Tuesdays, Thursdays, and Sundays, 9:00 am – 5:00 pm*

Tip: *Go on Sunday when the market is the best and busiest.*

#3: Pisac Market, Sacred Valley

It was a toss up between visiting Chinchero Market or Pisac Market. Pisac has a reputation of being very touristy while Chinchero Market is said to offer a more traditional experience.

While we did not visit Pisac Market, the market is popular for locally crafted wares and artisanal goods. The city is a picturesque Andean village, and the market takes place in the central square.

The main draw to this market is for the wide variety of handicraft, which local guides claim to be priced cheaper than at the markets in Cusco.

Location: *Pisac Market, Main Square Pisac*

Address: *Located about 28 kilometers from Cusco in the Sacred Valley*

Hours: *Tuesdays, Thursdays, Sundays, 9:00 am – 5:00 pm*

Tip: *Go on Sunday when the market is the best and busiest.*

Vendor with potatoes at Mercado Artesanal de Machu Picchu

#4: Mercado Artesanal de Machu Picchu

No doubt your trip to Cusco will include a visit to Machu Picchu. When you arrive into Aguas Calientes, the town near Machu Picchu, you'll walk right through the open-air Machu Picchu market as you leave the train station.

Among the products for sale are handicrafts, ceramics, jewelry, straw baskets, clothing made with *vicuña* and alpaca wool, accessories and more. On the second level of the market you'll find fruits, vegetables and a few food stalls.

Since you'll walk right through this market, take the time to explore it. Head upstairs for a less-touristy experience.

Location: *Mercado Artesanal de Machu Picchu*

Address: *Machu Picchu Pueblo*

Hours: *Open every day*

Tip: *Head upstairs for a more traditional experience.*

3. RESOURCES
What You Should Know About Traveling In Peru

CULINARY CULTURE IN PERU AND BEYOND
- Peruvian Chefs and Legends

HEALTH AND FITNESS WHILE TRAVELING IN PERU
- Altitude
- Trekking in Cusco
- Running in Lima

FROM OUR BLOG: MACHU PICCHU:
The Fulfillment of a Dream

Culinary Culture in Peru and Beyond

Peruvian Chefs & Legends

Food has made Peru one of the most important culinary destinations in the world. For a five-year streak from 2012 to 2016, Peru won the World's Leading Culinary Destination.

Many people have made and continue to make Peru a sought-after destination for its cuisine. In this section, we highlight three of the most influential chefs you will likely come across while planning for a trip to Peru.

However, it is important to give credit to the farmers who cultivate the land, the fishermen who harness the richness of the Pacific Ocean and lakes, and the diversity of natural products from the Andes regions and the Peruvian Amazon Jungle.

Gastón Acurio - Peruvian Food Ambassador

Gastón Acurio is regarded as the ambassador of Peruvian food culture. He has turned Peruvian cuisine into the country's proudest export. He is Peru's most well-known chef, with a restaurant empire spanning the globe. His restaurant, Astrid & Gastón, in Lima ranks 14th in the World's 50 Best Restaurants.

His franchise includes cookbooks, food festivals like Mistura, and restaurants at different price points and with different themes, making it accessible to a wide range of customers.

In his definitive Peruvian cookbook, Gastón Acurio guides you through the range of Peru's vibrant cuisine. Featuring over 500 traditional home cooking recipes, you will bring the flavors of Peru into your own kitchen.

Get the Book: Peru: The Cookbook by Gastón Acurio

Mitsuharu Tsumura - Nikkei Cuisine

Chef Mitsuharu Tsumura, who goes by "Micha," tells the story of his Japanese-Peruvian heritage through food. His restaurant, Maido, in Lima has an avant-garde *Nikkei* menu that mixes Peruvian ingredients with Japanese techniques and a touch of modern magic.

In 2016, Mitsuharu and Maido landed at number 13 on the coveted World's 50 Best Restaurants list (and number 2 in Latin America), winning the Highest Climber Award in the process.

Maido offers a fifteen-course meal, named the 'Nikkei Experience', that explores Peru's unique biodiversity, while incorporating the best food of both Peru and Japan.

Virgilio Martínez - Culinary Anthropologist

Peru's long history, indigenous groups, and robust immigrant population make it one of the most culturally diverse countries in Latin America.

Renowned Peruvian Chef Virgilio Martínez has collected a number of accolades for his use of Peruvian flora and fauna in creating unique dishes that pay tribute to Peru's traditions.

Virgilio Martínez is the chef and owner of Central Restaurante in Peru, which sits at number four on the World's 50 Best Restaurants list. In addition, he has a Michelin-starred restaurant called Lima in London and another outpost in Dubai.

The tasting menu at Central Restaurante is organized by the altitude, and takes you on a tour of the different regions of Peru, while celebrating the ingredients of each region. It is an attempt to give a holistic portrait of Peru's diverse ecology.

His cookbook, also named "**Central**," is organized in the same way. You can discover more about Peruvian ingredients and cuisine at the different altitudes through recipes, photos, and personal essays.

Get the Book: **Central by Virgilio Martínez**

Health and Fitness While Traveling in Peru

Health

There is nothing worse than getting ill while traveling. Unfortunately, this is something all travelers need to prepare for in advance. Peru offers high-level medical care at reasonable prices. You will find clinics around the country, with English-speaking medical staff, that cater to foreigners. However, the quality and availability of treatment can vary outside of the major tourist destinations.

To be on the safe side, we recommend purchasing travel insurance in advance. We personally use **World Nomads**, which provides great coverage for medical, dental, travel, and electronic equipment. In Peru, with the many natural herbs available, depending on your illness, locals may be able to provide natural alternatives to prescription pills. In the event that you need to seek medical treatment, be prepared to pay cash in advance for your treatments.

Altitude Sickness

If you're planning on visiting cities high above sea level, like Cusco and the Sacred Valley, be prepared for altitude sickness.

Cusco, the capital of the Inca Empire, sits at 11,200 feet (3,400 meters) above sea level. Altitude sickness, known as *soroche* in Peru, starts affecting most people at 8,000 feet or higher.

Altitude sickness affects everyone differently. Above 8,000 feet, the air is "thinner," meaning there is less pressure, so while the oxygen percentage remains the same, the air is less dense. Each breath you take contains less oxygen than what you're used to.

To counteract this, your body will at first breathe faster and pump blood more rapidly in order to take in the same amount of oxygen it is accustomed to receiving. For many this causes a variety of symptoms.

Some of the common symptoms include mild headaches, shortness of breath after moderate physical activity, like climbing stairs or walking around the city. More serious cases of altitude sickness can include nausea or vomiting, extreme fatigue, dizziness, loss of appetite and shortness of breath, even at rest.

To help cope with the effects, we've listed a number of ways below to help treat altitude sickness. The best way is to consult your doctor before leaving about prescribing altitude medications.

Treating Altitude Sickness

1. **Rest and take it easy.** More than likely the first thing you'll want to do when you arrive is walk around and explore. Keep in mind your body is trying to get accustomed to the lower amount of oxygen it's getting. Don't put any excess stress on your body as it is already working overtime to oxygenate your blood.
2. **Avoid alcohol.** Hold off on the pisco sours for the first couple of days you're in Cusco. Alcohol may exacerbate the effects of altitude sickness.
3. **Drink lots of water.** As you adjust to the change in altitude, dehydration can increase the symptoms of altitude sickness. The high elevations tend to be dry, so you'll probably need more water than you think.
4. **Drink coca tea**. Locals swear by it. This tea is however controversial. The leaves from the coca plant contain alkaloids, which when extracted chemically are the source for cocaine. However, the tea is totally safe to drink. Besides tea, you can also consume coca candy or simply chew on the leaves like the locals.
5. **Taking medication is also an option.** Consult your doctor on the best altitude sickness medication.

Fitness: Trekking in Cusco

Your travels through Peru will tempt you with an array of delicious and authentic flavors on a regular basis. This does not mean that you have to pack on unnecessary pounds or kilos.

Keeping fit is an important part of our food travels, and running is our favorite activity. Regardless of your fitness level, the easiest way to stay active in Peru is to simply put on your walking shoes and explore.

Cusco is a paradise for hiking. All around the historic city of Cusco are archeological marvels worth discovering. Some treks are shorter, some are longer and more difficult, while others are challenging multi-day treks, further away from the center of Cusco.

The best (and cheapest) way to visit the highlights of Cusco and the Sacred Valley is to buy a *Boleto Turístico del Cusco* (Cusco Tourist Ticket). This pass provides access to a number of archaeological sites in Cusco and the Sacred Valley, as well as five museums in Cusco.

Some of the sites are easily accessible from the center of Cusco, making for a great hike in the area. Others will require taking a *collectivo* (minibus), to hike at farther-flung Inca ruins.

Do keep in mind the high altitudes. Remember not to overexert yourself, and stay hydrated.

Where to Buy Your Tickets in Cusco
- Get your tickets in Cusco at the **COSITUC** office on 103 Avenida del Sol in the centre of Cusco. (www.cosituc.gob.pe)
- **Hours:** Monday to Friday 8:00am–6:30pm; Saturday, 8:00am –2:00pm

Fitness: Running in Lima

Beyond the eating, running is part of our daily routine. It not only keeps us in shape, but it is also a way to discover the local neighborhoods. Lima can be intimidating for runners. It is a busy city, with lots of traffic and sidewalks that are not always large enough to accommodate runners and pedestrians.

That said, you can always find places to run. For example, right next to where we were staying in Lince was a small public park with exercise equipment outdoors.

Park in the center of Lima

One of Lima's main roads, Avenue Arequipa, runs from the Miraflores district to downtown. Every Sunday the avenue is blocked off to traffic, and open for people exercising. The avenue extends from north to south for about three miles, passing through the districts of Lima, Lince, San Isidro and Miraflores. This was our favorite place to run, sharing the road with bikes, joggers and roller skaters on the wide streets.

The most popular destination for locals and tourists alike is along the Malecón bike path. This is a beautiful path on the waterfront that stretches from San Isidro through Miraflores past the Larcomar shopping centre and the Parque del Amor, all the way to Barranco district.

You can stick to the path or take the steps that descend to a sandy beach and run along the oceanfront path. Along the path are stations with exercise equipment, where you can incorporate strength training into your cardio activities.

Enjoy the tantalizing Peruvian cuisine on your travels. Eating your way through Peru does not mean that you should abandon your fitness regimen. Walk, run or use the public workout equipment and stay fit and healthy on your travels.

FROM OUR BLOG
MACHU PICCHU: THE FULFILLMENT OF A DREAM

For many years, Rosemary had dreamed about visiting Machu Picchu. Our trip to Cusco was not only for the food, but to also fulfill a childhood dream.

Machu Picchu, one of the Seven Wonders of the World, is a must-visit destination. When we arrived in Cusco on December 23rd, 2015, Rosemary's dream was about to become a reality. We decided to make the grand entrance into Machu Picchu on January 1st, 2016. But, little did we know we would run into several obstacles while getting the tickets: the saga is detailed in our blog.

In short, the ticket office would not sell the tickets in advance. We were told to pick them up at the last minute--a daunting arrangement when there were bus schedules and hotels to arrange! Panicking that we did not have our tickets by December 30th, we considered giving up our goal to be on the summit on the first day of the year. Rosemary, however, was not willing to give up her dream.

We woke up early on December 30th to buy the tickets online, then went to two locations to figure out how to pay for them in cash, and then we had to visit yet another location to have the tickets printed—only to have the printer break! But printer repaired and tickets in hand, we just barely caught our bus to begin the real journey.

As it is when it comes to achieving any dream, you are faced with many choices: give up, change plans, or keep pushing through. Rosemary persevered. She could hardly contain her excitement as she passed through the security checkpoints at the entrance of Machu Picchu on January 1st.

Machu Picchu is situated between two mountains: *Cerro* and *Huayana Picchu*. The best way to have a clear view of Machu Picchu is to admire it from the top.

Each step of the way, as she climbed from 2,400 meters up to the lofty summit of Cerro Machu Picchu at 3,061 meters, Rosemary reflected on how she almost pushed off her dream. The hike was surprisingly steep, and care is needed to find one's balance on large, slippery, uneven steps in the rain.

Each step for Rosemary was an analogy for life. Push through the obstacles. Sometimes, you know where you want to go, but cannot always see the clear path forward. Keep putting one foot in front of the other and stay focused.

The magnificent view from the top was nothing short of remarkable. Looking down and admiring the Inca ruins from the top and through the clouds was incredible.

Being at Machu Picchu was a truly an amazing experience. The construction, design and foresight of the Inca is remarkable. It's difficult to fathom how advanced they were at the time.

The experience was personal for Rosemary: it was a reminder to believe in your dreams, no matter how long it takes to achieve them.

(Read the full story at: **AuthenticFoodQuest.com***)*

ACKNOWLEDGEMENTS

"Certainly, travel is more than the seeing of sights; it is a change that goes on, deep and permanent, in the ideas of living."

– Miriam Beard, American Historian & Suffragist

The journey into Peru's culinary scene took a serendipitous turn when we signed up for private Spanish classes with Deborah Tveter in Chicago prior to our departure. Deborah not only taught us the language, but she also shared her love for Peruvian culture and gastronomy.

That fortuitous meeting led to our introduction to Cecilia Portella Morote, a gastronomy journalist in Lima. Through multiple conversations at various restaurants and food-related experiences, Cecilia and her friend, Mae Rivera, introduced us to the rich local Peruvian food scene.

In Lima, we met the gracious and generous Patricia Leonardo Torres. You were our amazing host in Lima, in the Lince Barrio. You shared your passion for Peruvian food generously. Not only did you offer recommendations and suggestions for what to do, but you also cooked and shared your favorite Peruvian dishes. And with your partner, Enrique, you taught us how to make a pisco sour, the national drink of Peru.

We would be remiss if we did not thank Doris Bustamante Ramirez and her family for opening up their home to us in Cusco. You welcomed us to share our first Peruvian Andean Christmas, and you guided us through the unique ingredients, grains and foods from Cusco and the Andes region. Our discussions about the food, the Inca heritage and the modern day Peruvian culture, gave us a broader appreciation of the culture and cuisine. Thank you for your openness and willingness to share.

To the chefs, cooks and experts we met on the road, thank you for sharing your passion for Peruvian cuisine. A special thanks to Sulma Penaherrera of El Bijao Restaurant, for introducing us to the fascinating Peruvian Amazon food and drinks. We also thank Chef Masa

Hamada at Tzuru Nikkei Restaurant for taking time out of your busy schedule to share your passion for Japanese-Peruvian cuisine. To Ivan at TK Restaurant in Lima, thank you for introducing us to the world of fusion Amazon cuisine.

We are very grateful to our friends and family who have supported us along this journey. Our heartfelt thanks to Genevieve Rouger and Catherine Ndegwa for believing in us. To Rose and Lori Hannigan, thank you for letting us call your home our home. To Emily Kidd, our editor, thank you for taking our words and making them sing.

Lastly, we give our gratitude to the Authentic Food Quest community. Your engagement, questions and desire to learn about authentic specialties fuels us, and it is as much your journey as it is ours.

ABOUT THE AUTHORS

"Once a year, go someplace you've never been before."

– **Dalai Lama**

Claire & Rosemary at La Cusqueñita Restaurant, Cusco

Rosemary Kimani and Claire Rouger started Authentic Food Quest in mid-2015. Their aim is to inspire people to travel through the local and authentic flavors of a destination. In doing so, they believe, travelers will have deeper and more meaningful experiences.

Traveling through food offers us a window into a country's culture and people. When you open up to a new flavors, tastes and textures, you learn a new aspect of the local culture. Through food, you develop bonds with the locals, and you grow, stretch and become transformed.

Leading from a sense of childlike curiosity, Rosemary and Claire follow their "Savor Local" process to help them discover the local and authentic flavors of a region. They travel around the world using food as their lens to discover a region. So far, their quest has taken them to South America and Southeast Asia, where they traveled slowly and lived with locals to better understand the local food culture.

When they are not on the road, they continue to explore the local flavors wherever they are based. So far, they have traveled to more than 35 countries and over 234 cities through food. They have created Authentic Food Quest to be a resource platform that connects travelers to local food experiences.

Rosemary and Claire are also authors of **Authentic Food Quest Argentina**, available on **Amazon** and **Barnes & Noble**.

Prior to Authentic Food Quest, Rosemary and Claire held senior level positions in corporate America. As a former advertising strategy director, Rosemary worked on global brands in the U.S. and France to develop compelling connections between brands and consumers. Claire holds a M.S. in Mechanical Engineering, as well as an MBA. She worked at Fortune 200 companies in the U.S. and France, with her most recent experience in food equipment manufacturing.

Now digital nomads, Rosemary and Claire seek to inspire travelers to travel deeper by opening up to the unique tastes, flavors and textures of a destination.

How do you explore the local food on your travels? What kind of experiences excite you the most about the food? Discover your food traveler profile and the unique experiences you should have when you take the **quiz on Authentic Food Quest**.

You can also connect with Rosemary and Claire at:
AuthenticFoodQuest.com

Facebook: www.facebook.com/AuthenticFoodQuest

Instagram: www.instagram.com/AuthenticFoodQuest

Twitter: **@afoodquest**

Pinterest: www.pinterest.com/afoodquest

Youtube: www.youtube.com/c/AuthenticFoodQuest

Savor The Adventure!

If you enjoyed the book, please take a few seconds to leave a review on Amazon.

A Note About Links

Please note that some of the links in this book might be affiliate links. If you purchase products through these links, we will get a small commission, at no cost to you. We only recommend products that we use or that we believe will be useful to you. If you choose to purchase using these links, we thank you in advance for your support to help us continue our quest for authentic food!

Also By Rosemary Kimani & Claire Rouger

Authentic Food Quest Argentina:
A Guide to Eat Your Way Authentically Through Argentina

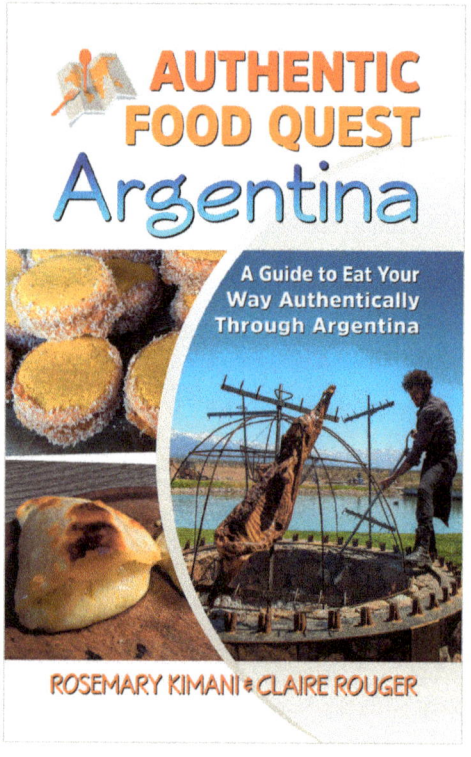

Available at Amazon and B&N.com

www.ingramcontent.com/pod-product-compliance
Lightning Source LLC
Chambersburg PA
CBHW051549010526
44118CB00022B/2632